Also by Derek Tangye and available in NEL paperbacks:

A DONKEY IN THE MEADOW
A CAT IN THE WINDOW
A CORNISH SUMMER
A DRAKE AT THE DOOR
A GULL ON THE ROOF

LAMA

Derek Tangye

Sketches by Jean Tangye

NEW ENGLISH LIBRARY
TIMES MIRROR

First published in Great Britain by Michael Joseph Ltd., in 1966
© by Derek Tangye 1966

*

FIRST NEL EDITION JUNE 1968
Reissued October 1971
New edition October 1974
This new edition February 1978

*

NEL Books are published by
New English Library Limited from Barnard's Inn, Holborn, London EC1N 2JR
Made and printed in Great Britain by Hunt Barnard Printing Ltd., Aylesbury, Bucks.

45003852 1

To the Mike Oliver family and their St Francis Home for
Animals at Porth, Newquay.

LAMA

1

I woke up on Christmas morning, looked out of the window across the wild boulder-strewn moorland to the turbulent white-capped sea of Mount's Bay, and was uncomfortably aware of the part I had to play.

'Merry Christmas!' I said cheerfully. Too cheerfully.

There was a second's silence.

'Merry Christmas!' said Jeannie, murmuring her greeting into the pillow.

Some people have no feeling for anniversaries. They consider a happy anniversary as a duty occasion when it is remembered in time, or an annoying one when it is remembered too late. They are unperturbed by sentimental anniversaries. They do not get bothered as some of us do by the thought: 'This time last year . . .'

The bedroom at Minack, our flower farm near Land's End, is very small. If you stand in the middle, holding the handle of a mop, you can touch each wall. There are two windows, each the size of a dinner plate when we arrived, but now enlarged so that they are casement windows; and one of them faces the moorland and the sea, and the other looks out on the square of grass which I call a lawn.

There is a William and Mary chest of drawers wedged between the foot of the bed and one of the rough faced, white-painted stone walls; and there is a small dressing table for Jeannie, and a little walnut desk like a school desk where she keeps her papers. There was also, under the bed, a contraption like a window frame except that wire mesh acted as a substitute for glass. It was a cunning device.

We had it made after Monty, of my book *A Cat in the Window*, the London cat we brought with us to Cornwall, had almost jumped into the jaws of a fox one night. I had awoken to the sound of Monty growling on the bed, instinctively put out a hand to grab him as he moved towards the window-sill, then a moment later switched on the torch, shone it into the dark outside, and was just in time to see a fox, the size of an Alsatian, gliding away up the lane.

Hence the wire meshed window frame. Just before we went to bed we used to fix it in the window; and so Monty was stopped from making dangerous nocturnal adventures while Jeannie and I continued to sleep with the window open. For eight months the contraption had remained unused under the bed.

'I'll get the tea!'

I proposed this easy way out to gain favour because I wanted to postpone the moment of present giving. I was unsure of myself. I had had Monty as a companion at every Christmas since Jeannie and I had married; and there had been a ritual, one of those foolish family rituals, in which Monty and I took Jeannie's presents to her together. And those that I gave her, and those that I provided Monty to give her, were accompanied by badly rhymed, well meant verses possessing some immediately topical personal aspect. Occasionally such verses gained greater applause than the presents themselves.

We have only the one living room. When we first came to the cottage the floor was of earth covered by thin, rat eaten boarding; and the first night we slept in it, we had brought Monty down in the car for the weekend, we lay on a mattress listening to the rain dripping from the roof, and in the morning there was a puddle in the middle of the room. It was a contrast to the night before, when Jeannie had entertained the American Ambassador and A. P. Herbert in her offices at the Savoy; and yet the cottage, in her mind, was like Aladdin's Cave. She had sensed it from the first moment, during a holiday we had spent at Lamorna, that she saw it. We had walked westwards along a tortuous cliff path from Lamorna Cove, then in a steep climb to a point called Carn Barges; and when we had reached the top we looked inland and saw the cottage half hiding in the trees a mile away. 'There it is!' cried Jeannie pointing towards it. There was never any doubt in either of our minds that however difficult the task might prove to be, the little cottage was going to be our home; and that its security once gained would make us, in our personal view, the luckiest, happiest couple in the world.

At one end of the living room was my kidney-shaped Regency desk which my father and mother had given me for a wedding present. It had travelled with us; first to Cholmondley House below Richmond Bridge, then to Thames Cottage where the boat race ends at Mortlake, and now to Minack, an ancient crofter's home where the walls of the cottage have foundation rocks which clamber up from the soil. And close to my desk there is a gap we had cut through the feet thick walls which gave us the entrance to the spare bedroom and the bathroom. We had bought the spare bedroom as a chicken house. It is still in reality a chicken house, though it is disguised now by the cedar wood panels which cover the outside.

At the other end of the room is the slow burning anthracite day and night stove. There was an ancient Cornish range in its place when we first came to Minack, rusty and unused for years; and we ripped it out and substituted a small coal stove and did most of the cooking on primitive paraffin heaters. Then, when Jeannie and I received a small legacy, we had installed our present stove, and, in this take-it-for-granted press-button age, I recommend the sweet pleasure enjoyed when, for the first time, one awakes in the morning to find the stove alight, the kettle aboil. It becomes, so it seems, one of the original pleasures.

There was, therefore, no delay in providing Jeannie with her tea. I poured a little of the milk which we collect from the farm at the top of the hill into the cup, filled the rest of it from the pot, then took it to her.

'What,' I asked in mock seriousness as I did so, 'would you like as a Christmas present?'

I expected the reply. I knew exactly what she wanted, but she was not going to get it.

'I want a kitten,' she replied, laughing at me, aware that my question was a game.

2

I WAS A cat hater before Monty came into my life. I hated all cats whether Siamese, Persian, Manx, tabby, torsoiseshell or alley. I came from a family of cat haters where cats were considered vulgar, ill-mannered, noisy, unhealthy and incapable of loving the human race as did the easily trained, dutiful dog. Cats, if they were unfortunate enough to come within sight of any member of our family, were quickly shooed off as if they were vermin.

My antipathy to cats was therefore ingrained. Then as I grew up and found to my surprise that homes as normal as mine actually enjoyed their company, I reacted in an extravagant way which in retrospect I know was a pose. If a cat came into a room where I was a guest, I behaved as if a whiff of poison gas had come with it. I would explode like a neurotic invalid. 'Take it away,' I would cry to my astonished hostess, 'my asthma! I can't breathe. Cats always have this effect on me!' I had read somewhere that a few people *were* affected by the presence of cats.

This was, in fact, how I behaved the first time Jeannie invited me to her home for her parents to inspect me. I had determined to be on my best behaviour and I arrived punctually for tea at their house in St Albans, welcomed at the door by Jeannie. 'Don't worry,' she said, smiling, 'Daddy's already got the drinks ready, tea or no tea.'

As it turned out, it was to be 'no tea'. I had no sooner sat down in my chair, engaged on a line of safe talk, a plate of thin bread and butter on a small table beside me, my cup of tea there too, when a huge blue Persian appeared from nowhere and jumped on to my lap. My good intentions and my good manners were forgotten. I uttered a yell. 'Take it away! Take it away!' And as I shouted I flayed my arms, the cat was sent flying, and the table beside me along with the bread and butter and the cup of tea was sent flying as well. This unhappy introduction prompted Jeannie's mother to say to Jeannie after I had gone: 'I don't quite know, dear, how you would get on married to a cat hater.'

For Jeannie, in her young life, had had a succession of cats of whom Tim, the blue Persian, was the reigning one. Cats, as I was now to learn, enveloped her as my family were enveloped by dogs. True she and her family had room for dogs too, Scottish terriers being their speciality, but cats had for her a particular virtue, a strange subtlety, an untouchable allure which was to me incomprehensible. I comprehended, however, that I had made a bloomer.

We married; and within three months forces were at work to persuade me to accept a cat into our home. At this stage, in view of what is going to happen, I think I should say that there was a chink in my armour as far as one type of cat was concerned. The black cat. Somewhere in my childhood an incident of much good fortune must have occurred involving the presence of a black cat. I have no recollection as to what it might have been. All I can say is that all my life I have had a lilt in my heart when a black cat has crossed my path. It never appeared to me as an animal in that I said to myself: 'Look, there's a black cat!' It was just a shadow wishing me good luck, a dart which struck my superstitious Cornish nature. Time and again, at moments of unsureness, the fleeting sight of a black cat in front of me had been the source of unreasonable comfort.

I had no chance to stop Monty entering my life. It was

unthinkable to Jeannie and her mother that I should behave so absurdly towards cats; and they deemed it certain that my prejudices would collapse if I were presented with a *fait accompli*. They thus plotted, and four months after our wedding day I was forced to accept the fact that a kitten had become a member of our household. A ginger kitten whose fur, when he became older, had the colour of autumn bracken.

I did for a time put on a show of indifference. I insisted, for instance, that it should be a kitchen cat; and whenever it strayed into another room at our cottage beside the Thames at Mortlake, I drove it back to where I believed it should belong. This attitude, this display of a dying independence, began to soften when I realised that Monty, small as he was, appeared to like me. Against my will I felt flattered. Here I was, the arch hater of his fraternity, being wooed by the most bewitching tricks. As if he had been informed by Jeannie to behave in this particular manner, he followed me about upsetting himself from time to time, displaying his buff underpants, softly clawing the finger with which I was lured to tickle him. Within a month I was ready to admit to Jeannie that Monty amused me. She had, in fact, caught Monty on my Regency desk, me with a pipe cleaner having a boxing match with his tiny paws; and I was laughing uproariously.

'Be careful he doesn't knock over the ink,' said Jeannie, not wishing to press her victory.

In the years that followed, Monty became an anchor in a restless life. Both Jeannie and I flashed here and there hugely enjoying ourselves, living the pace of two people who had the opportunity to taste that kind of life which others, more humdrum in their luck, envied. In due course, as the gaiety and the parties repeated themselves like a film seen a dozen times over, we began to see sense and that flippancy possesses no foundation. Later, when the lesson had at last penetrated, we decided to build a new life in Cornwall. In the meantime it was Monty, as I now realis   who gave us the balance. Both of us looked forward to seeing him, waiting for us alone in the cottage, as we lived gaily yet dangerously through the day.

MONTY DIED on a May morning in his sixteenth year. After his seven haphazard years in London, he lived the rest of his life corralled blissfully at Minack. Minack is a mile from the main road, along a bumpy, pot-ridden lane which, after reaching a scattering of farm buildings, leads nowhere except down the hill to the cottage. There is a wood edging away from the old grey stones of the cottage and, when first we came, there was a swamp beside it which we now have drained, building a greenhouse on the dry land. Away from the wood and the cottage, to the right as you look up the lane, a path runs a hundred yards to a large field then across and downwards to the top of the cliff. The cliff is steep but full of small meadows, hidden by high hedges, and which we created from the undergrowth when first we set out to build our flower farm. And far below are the rocks where gulls ruminate, and oyster catchers pipe, and cormorants stretch out their wings to dry, and curlews gather in gaunt groups, and the sea murmurs on still days.

Monty, as a country cat, marvelled at the change in his circumstances. He no longer had to sit in the window, staring glumly, waiting by himself for hour upon hour, wondering whether Jeannie and I would ever come home. The lonely part of his life was suddenly over. In London a neglected cat; in Cornwall a cat who, he may have thought sometimes, received too much attention. For here were the three of us together in uninterrupted companionship day and night.

Some enjoy the hallucination that if you tear up one part of your life and substitute another, congenial to your imagination, that you become immune to trouble. There is the gay, hopeful belief that if you can steel yourself to surrender the tedious, or tense, routine of life to which you have reluctantly become accustomed, problems inward and outward will dissolve. They do not. There is no such act as escapism. Wherever you go, whatever you do – emigrate, change jobs, find the dream cottage, pursue your true ambition – you have yourself as a companion; you have the same grim fight to earn a living. What you do gain, if you have the luck of Jeannie and me, is the chance to embrace an environment which you love, and which softens the blows when they come; for the expanse of sky helps to free us; so also the sense that the wild animals, the foxes, the badgers, have been going their mysterious ways for centuries; and the sea is as it always was. The reward, if you have the luck, is to become aware again that values have never changed, that true pleasure is as it has been since the beginning, that man is nobler than the bee. The aim to be free does not lie in association with the herd, for the herd has not the patience to probe. One has to delve into one's secret self. No one else can help. But if one lives in the environment of one's choice the task is made easier, the mind is more willing to explore.

So here were the three of us, each experimenting with a new kind of life; and there is no doubt that Monty's experiments were immediately successful. His hunting was no longer restricted to that of a rare indoor mouse; for to his amazement he discovered that he now lived in a world of mice. Mice in stone hedges, mice in hollows of trees, mice in waving grass, mice which came out of holes within tufts of turf. All kinds of mice. Tasty mice, mice big and small. Here he was in a realm of endless excitement, a huge area where he could wander always alert for the pounce. No need to wait unduly for the kill. A profusion of mice tempted him. He was a trout fisherman when the Mayfly are about.

And there were the rabbits. The first time he ever caught a baby rabbit he brought it to me as I sat at my desk, depositing it at my feet, announcing it with a jungle cry. And because I praised him foolishly with much enthusiasm, he thought I was pleased and for ever afterwards he was bringing rabbits to my feet. Pen in hand, unfinished letter before me, I would go through the formula of congratulating him. He seldom ate the rabbit which I would pick up and throw outside into some distant undergrowth.

He never hunted birds. Never at any time of his life did I see him show any interest whatsoever in stalking a bird; and while he was at Minack he developed a strange friendship with a chaffinch and a robin. Tim the robin used to sit indoors on the back of the chair on the seat of which Monty was sitting; and Charlie the chaffinch time and again hopped about the flower shed in daffodil time while Monty, dozily sitting on a bench, would take his presence for granted. It was strange, when Lama came, that she should behave in the same way towards birds.

He hated dogs, a maddening rage would seize him as soon as he saw one loping up the lane to the cottage; and this fixation was due, I believe, to an incident that occurred when he was very young. Our home at Mortlake was bombed, and we went to stay with Jeannie's parents at St Albans. They had a Scottie called Judy and when she was introduced to Monty in the drawing room, she made a snarling dash at Monty who, in his terror, shot up the curtains and ended up on the pelmet with fur upright. During the rest of his stay there was a continuous warfare, and peace could only reign if they were kept separated; and so Monty spent most of his stay at St Albans locked in a room. You might have thought that the effect of this would result in him being scared of dogs. Instead it created in him this rage

19

towards them. He would attack, not run away. And many a time a misguided dog owner seeing us run out of the cottage shouting: 'Look out for the cat!', replied by saying in a superior way: 'No need to worry . . . my dog doesn't chase cats.'

Monty was splendid to look upon, a head like a miniature tiger, fine whiskers, fat jowls, and a thick semi-Persian coat of rich red gold. Seldom did anyone passing through Minack fail to stop to admire him. He was so magnificent that he compelled admiration. He would sit musing on a rock, tail gently flicking, eyes half closed, listening disdainfully to the praise. And there was many a time when Jeannie and I would call to each other: 'Look at Monty' . . . just for the sheer pleasure of looking at him.

He had not, however, converted me into a cat worshipper. Of course I had learnt to notice other cats, just as one notices the makes of cars on long journeys, but in all the years with Monty I never became a cat worshipper like Jeannie; for in her eyes any old cat merited a coo and the wordy rigmarole associated with cat worshippers. My cat devotion was for Monty himself. He was my companion at Minack as a dog might have been, and the emotion that came to me when he died was the same as anyone feels for someone who has shared many adventures. I had no desire to replace him. I had no intention of doing so. A substitute could not be found for Monty, as one might find a replacement for a broken chair. My only wish was to have comfortable memories of him. A period of my life was over, and I would be for ever grateful for the happiness he had given me, and for the sympathy I had gained by his presence in troubled times. Monty, as far as I was concerned, was irreplaceable; and that was that.

But in the evening of the day he died, I said something to Jeannie which was not prompted by sense. The words came out of me as if I were wanting them to be a pillar against which I could lean. A wild hope hidden in a conundrum. An impulse from my subconscious. A sop to our sadness. I am quite sure there was not a flicker of reason behind them.

'On one condition only will I ever have a cat again,' I said boldly to Jeannie, 'and that is if a black cat comes to the cottage in a storm . . . and we never can find where it came from.'

Defensive words. No well meaning person was going to be made welcome who came to us saying: 'I hear you've lost your cat. I am very sorry, so would you like this kitten?' None of that. I was going to remain loyal to Monty. I was going to cherish the years he had given us.

I was going to prove it was true that I was a cat man.

'I want a kitten!' Jeannie had said that Christmas morning.

Not a chance.

4

I OF COURSE did not know I was being watched. I had met
people on occasions, those who possessed a special dotti-
ness for cats, who claimed that as soon as a cat vacancy
occurred it was broadcast cat fashion to all members of the
local fraternity. Soon after Monty had died, for instance, I
had met a sweet old lady in Penzance who said to me in a
tone of irritating certainty, a charming, knowing smile
pressing the point home: 'Don't you be upset about your
Monty, Mr Tangye. Next on the list will soon be with you!'

'Rubbish,' I replied, under my breath.

As the months passed after Monty died it was arguable
whether I was justified in maintaining my sense of loyalty
towards him. Jeannie's devotion to him had been no less
than mine, in fact more so; and yet she was prepared to
introduce another cat to Minack. Why not me? I had no
reasonable answer but I continued to say a sharp no whenever Jeannie mentioned the prospect. There was no Christmas spirit about me as far as this matter was concerned.

We now had Jane and Shelagh working on the flower
farm. Each of them had started with us when they were fourteen, and they belonged to the wild cliffs on which we lived
as the crying gulls belonged. Jane with fair, shoulder length
hair, who padded barefoot about her work at Minack during
the summer months. Shelagh, so introspective, a gentle cup
of a face, a waif. These two, I look back upon and know,
were part of the truest period of our life at Minack. I see
them now lugging the baskets of flowers up from the

meadows, or at the packing bench bunching daffodils as fast as they could, or on hot summer days patiently, yet always enthusiastically, planting drooping wallflower plants, hundred upon hundred of them, into a parched field. I laugh also when I think of them. They were always allies of Jeannie's in any matter concerning me, those mock, joking occasions which spice a working day.

'Let's hide the shovel and see him getting cross!'

'I'm going to tell him the violets were killed in the frost last night . . . then watch his face when we show him the baskets!'

'Keep out of his way . . . the tractor won't start!'

They were Jeannies allies, too, about gaining a successor to Monty. In the weeks which followed Christmas, as the flower harvest gathered speed, these two would share with Jeannie, a nudging, persistent, humorous campaign to make me change my mind. Almost every day, pretence or true, one of them would announce: 'I know of a kitten you can have!' And if it were Shelagh, she would add because she was always careful: 'It's free!'

And while we were laughing we were being watched.

The first news of this came one afternoon while Jeannie's mother was staying with us. It was the last week in February, the period when the flower harvest is rushing towards its climax, and the meadows are massed with bed upon bed of daffodil buds; and we are not interested in anything except picking, bunching, packing, and rushing to catch the flower train at Penzance. I scarcely listened when Jeannie's mother recounted her story. It certainly had no significance as far as I was concerned. It was just an incident on a walk.

For the first time she had brought Angus, her Scottie, with her. Angus had always been banned from Minack while Monty was alive, for Monty would never have allowed him into the cottage. He was a cheerful little dog, successor to Judy who had chased Monty up the curtains and on to the pelmet at St Albans; and because his home was a flat in London, Angus treated his walks around Minack as those in paradise. On this occasion he and his mistress had taken a walk to Pentewan meadows, meadows which we rented from our neighbour, and in which we grew potatoes as well as daffodils. When we gave up growing potatoes, we gave up Pentewan; and although the daffodil bulbs still lie in its soil we no longer can pick the flowers. Our original neighbour has sold his farm.

Jeanne's mother returned from this walk, and as always when she was excited her trifle Scottish accent became delightfully pronounced.

'Did you know you have a little black cat on your land? Angus chased it, he did. Right through the daffodils at the top of the big field, and the wee thing disappeared over the hedge into the moor.'

My only reaction, an instinctive annoyance, was that such a chase should not have been allowed to happen in the daffodil beds.

We were earning a living, we couldn't risk damage. Why wasn't Angus called off the chase?

But, as had happened once before when Monty came into my life, Jeannie's mother knew better. A damaged daffodil did not compare in value to a little black cat.

'Such a pretty wee thing it was,' she said; and looked at me.

5

JEANNIE'S MOTHER slept in the chicken house, the chicken house we had bought to serve as a spare room. One half of its roof sloped towards the field at the back of the cottage, so that the gutter was almost level with the grass.

On one occasion when she was staying with us she was awakened by a noisy, clumsy clambering on the roof. At first she thought it was a man trying to break into the cottage, and she lay quite still. It was a full moon, and after a few minutes of her heart beating fast, she fingered the gingham curtains aside and looked out. At that moment a shadow jumped from the roof, and as it landed she realised what it was that had startled her from her sleep. A fox.

In the morning she recounted this incident to Jeannie and me, in the same mood of seriousness as she had met it. Then, after a moment's pause so that one actually saw the thought going through her, she looked at me, smiling and said: 'He thought I was an old chicken.'

Angus on this visit, his first visit, slept on a rug draped in a small armchair which my own mother had given us when we first came to Minack. He had no wish to sleep for long, the gorgeous extent of his holiday was so wonderful that every second had to be experienced; and as we were always up as the pale sun stretched from the Lizard through the window of our bedroom, we used to open the door and let him out. Jeannie's mother was also usually awake; and she would say in the manner of someone glad to be the witness of pleasure: 'Go on Angus, go for a walk, have a good time!'

On this particular morning Jeannie went straight into the packing shed to begin packing the flowers we had picked and bunched the day before; and I took Angus for a quick run down the path to the big field, then right, towards the Pentewan meadows. I was on my way back, Angus ahead of me, when he suddenly barked, then ears back, stumpy tail upright, he set off in a fussy gallop. I saw him disappear round the bend into the big field, and I knew he was making for the daffodil beds again. I ran after him, uselessly shouting, and when I reached the gap that led to the field he had already reached the far hedge; and with legs too short to give him a chance to jump up it, he was revenging his impotence by barking furiously. I had seen no sign of his quarry.

'What was Angus barking about?' asked Jeannie when I got back to the packing shed, 'did he see the little black cat again?'

'*He* may have done,' I said, showing no enthusiasm, 'I didn't.'

Angus and his mistress went back to London a day or two later, and there were no more chases before he left. But in the afternoon of the day they had gone, Shelagh, who had been picking wallflowers in a meadow overlooking the sea, called the skol meadow, arrived back in the packing shed in high excitement.

'I've just seen the little black cat!' she said breathlessly, 'I surprised it asleep in the wallflowers, and it ran away and dashed down the badger hole in the corner!'

'The badger hole?' I murmured. There was a notorious sett at one end of the skol meadow. Then I added, meaning to annoy: 'A nice meal for a badger anyhow.'

'How heartless he is, Mrs Tangye,' said Jane, busily bunching, with a mock heavy sigh.

Jeannie, of course, behaved predictably. She was standing alongside Jane bunching posies . . . a collection of wall-flowers, forget-me-nots, anemones, freesias, all beautifully arranged and which we marketed proudly as Cornish Posies.

'I'm going straight away to look for it,' she said, hurriedly finishing a bunch. And off she went.

She found nothing, but the incident had introduced a new zest into the flower season. And while I remained humourless, enmeshed in the mechanics of prices, making fanciful calculations of what we might earn the following week and the week after, worrying whether or not when it was all over we would have enough in the bank to keep us going, the little black cat began to imprint its personality on Minack. It was no longer a black dash. It began discreetly to position itself in sight of us.

Thus, as March advanced, the chatter tended to concentrate on its activities. Jane and Shelagh would bring in their flowers to the shed, unload them from the baskets, putting them in galvanised pails or glass jars according to their varieties; and then start bunching those that had already been in water for twenty four hours.

'I saw it this morning.'

'So did I.'

'Where?'

'As I was bicycling down the lane,' said Shelagh, 'just this side of the well.'

Shelagh lived in the village of St Buryan, four miles from Minack. Jane's cottage was one of three which stood poised beside the glorious Pentewan cliffs; and it has been empty, like its neighbours, since Jane left. She lived there with her mother, a young brother, a white cat, a lamb, a budgerigar, a griffin, a bull terrier, and any creature which momentarily required love. The cottage was two fields away from Minack.

'Joe,' announced Jane one day, 'says he's seen it in the quarry.'

Joe worked for the same farmer as her mother. I had known him since we came to Minack, a skilled shoveller, an expert on cliff potatoes, a countryman, a true representative of a dying race. An observer of small incidents.

'Did he say anything about it?' The first occasion I had shown interest.

Only that he's seen it a number of times, but never further from Minack than the quarry.'

The quarry was extinct. Once upon a time it provided the blue elvin stone which served as a base for many of the lanes around St Buryan. It was small, and above the lower Pentewan meadows. It also marked our farthest boundary.

'You see,' said Jane, smiling at me, 'the cat never goes further west than the quarry, nor further east than the well. Never strays from your land.'

The cat quite clearly was closing in on me. At the same time, so absorbed was I with mundane matters, that I was not truly conscious of what was happening. Then as I went about my business, I began to notice saucers left in odd places; and sometimes they were empty. I also realised that the cat was now being regularly seen and it was no longer a sensational piece of news to announce. I saw it myself, several times, at the far end of the stable meadow through the packing shed window. What was more significant I began to sense that there was a conspiracy against me; and that the cat had these powerful allies of Jeannie, Jane and Shelagh. There was developing an uncomfortable atmosphere that once again I was the odd man out.

'Stop courting the cat,' I said one day crossly, after the post had brought details of bad prices and I was about to take another load of flowers to the station, 'it's never going to live here and it's selfish of you to deceive it.' I started the Land Rover and drove off; but disquietingly I noticed that the three of them said nothing. Heads down, they continued with their work.

They were plotting. As soon as they saw the back of the Land Rover disappearing up the lane, they would laugh amongst each other; and make their plans.

6

THE CAT, however, was not co-operating. I was quite sure of this. Had they been able to approach it, had it shown any sign of yielding to their blandishments, they would have trumpeted news of their victory. Instead there was a scheming silence. Saucers continued to be left half way up the lane. Others were placed on the path down to the big field. And all this seemed to add up to the fact that the cat was not ready to accept them.

The first person who touched it was me.

We kept a few chickens in those days, and their home was a house in the wood. They had a good run and it was surrounded by wire mesh netting to protect them from marauding foxes and badgers. One early morning when I went there to open up their door, I found the cat outside awaiting me. It did not wait long. It had one terrified look at me, then bolted across the run to the far side.

One's life is littered with actions not governed by the intellect, and much is gained thereby. Time and again in my own life I would have been left standing in a backwater, had I allowed my mind coolly to appraise a situation; and the same thing would have happened now, had I permitted logic to decide. Up to now I had crossly condemned the antics of Jane, Shelagh and Jeannie to court the cat. Yet here I was rushing across the run in pursuit of it.

When I reached the other side, the cat was battering itself frantically against the wire netting, plunging its little head into one of the holes as if by so doing it could squeeze its body through to safety. My presence only made it plunge the more frantically.

I instinctively put out my hand to stop it, and momentarily my fingers clasped the bony, thin little body. Then terror really seized it. It raced away from me, leapt on to the top of the chicken house, from there to a branch, then another leap over the top of the wire, and away into the depths of the wood.

I was, nevertheless, one up on the others. All their talk and they had not been even within a few feet, let alone touch it. The situation titillated me. My ego was flattered. I now had a story to tell them which would compel envy. Light hearted envy, of course.

'How is your dear little cat?' I said innocently, when they were all gathered together in the packing shed.

'Why do you ask?' said Shelagh suspiciously.

'Just wondered.'

'He's up to something,' Jane was looking across to Jeannie. 'I feel it. There's a look in his eye which means trouble. Has he told you anything, Mrs Tangye?'

'Nothing,' said Jeannie.

'I certainly don't mean trouble,' I said, 'but I've got something to boast about. I've *touched* your little black cat.' And I proceeded to tell them the story.

A few days earlier another event had occurred which provided a bizarre coincidence. On the day before Monty had died, Jeannie had had a fanatical desire to paint him. She knew he had only a few hours to live, and she believed she would be happier if she remembered these moments on canvas. Just as she was finishing the picture, a picture which now hangs on the wall of the sitting room, she ran out of paint. There were still three faint orange stripes to do on his forehead, and she was at a loss how to manage them. Then she suddenly had a bright idea. We were growing that year a meadow of orange marigolds which we were using in the

Cornish Posies; and Jeannie ran out to the meadow, a meadow beside the path which took us to Pentewan, and picked a handful. She came back to the cottage, plucked some petals from the cup of a marigold, then rubbed them on the canvas. They produced exactly the right colour.

We had left the marigolds to grow for another year in the same meadow; and there I was walking along the path towards Pentewan when I saw, out of the corner of my eye, that I was being observed. A tiny black head, two little ears, and a pair of slit amber eyes, almost hidden in the blaze of marigolds, followed my person as I passed. It was a weird experience because under this scrutiny I felt almost self-conscious, as if I had discovered I was being secretly assessed for a job. It was not until later that I remembered about Jeannie and Monty's marigold petals.

There was soon to be the other coincidence. It is, of course, convenient to call anything a coincidence which cannot be rationally explained. It is comforting, in this age when men like to think their plans can control the future, to dismiss the unexplainable as a coincidence. It is a reassurance that man, in his time on earth, is still the omnipotent force his ego needs to imagine himself to be. Hence I call the final entrance into my life of the little black cat as a coincidence.

A few hours after Monty had died I had made that strange remark to Jeannie. I had said that I myself would never have another cat because my cat loyalty was only to Monty; the sort of remark people often make when an animal dies with whom they have shared the experiences of years. But I had added, you remember, that I would make an exception if a black cat whose home we could never trace, came to the door of Minack in a storm.

On Easter Sunday, a week or so after the incidents of the marigold meadow and that of the chicken run, a tremendous storm blew up from the south. The rain and the gale swept in from the sea, roaring against the cottage, so that inside we had to raise our voices in order to hear each other.

There was a pause in our conversation. Jeannie was sitting in the armchair in front of the stove, and she was a little upset because she was reading her diary of the year before. Quite unreasonably she was feeling that she could have done more for Monty in his illness than she had done. A common belief of those who have loved.

Suddenly I said: 'Did you hear that?'

Quite distinctly I heard a sound which was strange to the wild noises of a storm. It was a miaow.

'*Something* I heard,' said Jeannie.

I got up from the sofa where I had been sitting, and went over to the door, and part of the storm came into the room when I opened it; and so did the little black cat.

7

WE PUT it on the bed that first night, and left the window
open. We thought, after sleeping off the huge meal Jeannie
had given it, that it might regret its decision to enter the
cottage; and so we left it free to escape if it wished. But it
never moved. Instead a friend came through the window to
visit it. I was lying awake when it arrived, and saw the
shadow on the sill.

'Jeannie!' I shouted as I switched on the torch, 'our black
cat is a girl. Sammy from the farm has just jumped in through
the window!'

We had never investigated. We were so affected by the
magic which had brought it to Minack that we had taken
it for granted that it was male. I had never thought in terms
of a female cat. My mind only associated itself with the
gorgeous male which was Monty.

'You're right!' cried Jeannie.

The light of the torch shone on a crouching figure, a foot
away from the bottom of the bed. Sammy, an active sandy
tom, notorious for his wanderings in the neighbourhood.

'Psst!' I hissed as fiercely as I could. Not a move.

'Get out!' I shouted.

But Sammy, either too frightened to budge or too
influenced by the charms of Lama, remained still. I then
picked up a glass of water beside the bed, and cruelly flung
its contents at him. He disappeared through the window.

'Well,' I said as I got up and shut the window after him,
'this is awful. Supposing the cat is going to have kittens?'

'Let's go to sleep.'

'It's all very well,' I said, 'but this puts a very different complexion on the situation. We don't want kittens all over the place.'

'*You* don't?'

'All right I don't. I never visualised having more than one cat. You see . . . '

'Stop arguing. Talk about it in the morning.'

The little black cat, meanwhile, had remained quite undisturbed throughout this activity. She was dead to the world. She had consumed, prior to being carried to bed by Jeannie, a large saucer of bread and milk, a liberal portion of the chicken we were having for dinner, and a slice of the liver from the morrow's dinner. She lay in a tight ball at the bottom of the bed, dreaming perhaps that her feast was a dream.

And as she dreamt I roamed my selfish thoughts over the merits of having another cat. Of being tied again. We had nothing dependent upon us at Minack at this time except the few chickens, and the wild birds, and Hubert the gull; and Jane and Shelagh could look after them. There was no Boris the drake then, or Penny and Fred the donkeys. We were free to go away without tedious and elaborate plans to cover our absence; or more accurately perhaps I should say I *felt* free to go away.

I was facing the old challenge of having to decide the degree of worthwhileness in giving up a part of one's independence; and that in itself is a selfish remark. One is flotsam if there is no sacrifice. The belief that personal freedom is obtained by cutting the shackles is an illusion. The pure happiness exists when the mainstream represents the base one has struggled for; but the edge is provided by the giving. Even to a cat.

In the morning Jeannie said she would take the Land Rover and telephone the vet. We do not have a telephone.

34

When people want us urgently they send us a telegram, asking us to ring them; and that means we are protected from those who would ring us on the spur of the moment. When we ourselves want to telephone, we drive a couple of miles to a phone box. Or we go to the Queens Hotel in Penzance where Jeannie used to stay with her parents year after year before going to the Scillies; and where Billy and Frank looked after them, as they look after Jeannie and me now.

The vet, the quiet Scotsman, in due course arrived. When he entered the cottage the little black cat, like a snarling tigress, shot away to a corner of the room. She had gone wild again.

'Come now,' he said in his soft accent, 'nothing to worry about. Let me have a look at you.'

She was under a bookcase behind my desk.

'Look at this liver,' coaxed Jeannie, proffering the saucer and the dark pieces thereon, 'delicious . . . you loved it last night!'

The shadow, merging with the old, feet thick stone walls of the cottage, was not to be bribed.

'Come on, come on,' said the vet very softly as if he were caressing her, 'you're safe with me, you know.'

She did not agree. Each time one of us approached her she dashed to another part of the room, then crouched there, fur upright, spitting at us, blazing with rage.

The vet smiled. 'I don't see you keeping her for long,' he said, 'she's so wild that only a zoo could keep her.'

In the end it was Jeannie who cornered her, and picked her up savagely squeaking, struggling, ready to scratch her way free again.

'Shut up!' she said firmly. And miraculously she shut up.

'That's certainly a victory for you,' said the vet, 'now come on, see if you can't be the same with me.'

She sullenly let it be so. I watched the smouldering yellow eyes as the vet prodded her.

'I don't think she's more than three months old,' he said, 'and if I were you I'd let me take her back to the surgery. In a week you can collect her, and there won't be any toms to go after her again.'

A week later we did collect her. She was in a basket, the same basket we bought for Monty when he first came to Minack. We reached the top of Boleigh Hill, then turned left into the lane which leads to Minack.

And as we did so, from out of the basket there came a great volume of purrs.

8

WE CALLED her Lama. The Dalai Lama was escaping from Tibet at the time of her arrival at Minack. 'DALAI LAMA SAFE' we read in a headline one day, and cut it out of the paper and stuck it on a beam in the stables. A suitable name we therefore thought. And, in view of the link with Monty, a symbolic name.

The night that she came back from the vet, she had jumped on the bed, put her head on Jeannie's shoulder and stayed there the night through, periodically bursting into purrs.

'I've got cramp.'

'Turn over then.'

'I can't.'

'Why?'

'Lama's so comfortable.'

'Oh Heavens,' I said, 'so this game has started all over again.'

I don't mind admitting that I had greatly enjoyed the interval during which I had slept in comfort. Night hours and night hours during Monty's lifetime I had spent with limbs numbed while Monty lay against a leg or a foot, blissfully asleep at my expense. And now the performance was scheduled to start again.

'Don't you think,' I said gently, 'that it might be a good idea to have a new regime with Lama? After all she's been accustomed to sleep in any old place.'

'I can't wait to see *you* pushing her off the bed.'

Jeannie's knowledge of me was, of course, quite correct. The discomfort, the readiness for self-sacrifice, had always received its compensation when I stretched out my hand and touched a paw, or traced a finger on a forehead; for Monty all his life had provided me with reassurance during dismal wakes in early mornings, and now Lama could do the same. I was, therefore, defeating myself if I were so selfish as to try to ban her from a portion of the bed.

'Well,' I said, 'you're probably right.'

There was a pause.

'Lama,' murmured Jeannie, 'you've won.'

On reflection I find the strangest feature of Lama's advent was our certainty that she would stay. We never had any qualms that she was only using us as a hotel, having a rest and feeding herself up before moving on to somewhere else or going back to where she came from. And we were silently cross with those who prophesied that we would soon be alone again.

'I know all about these wandering cats,' said a friend importantly who had three cats, 'they simply live with you for a while, take all your attention, and just when you have become fond of them off they go.'

'I had a cat,' said another, 'which came to our door in a starving condition just like yours and stayed three months. We were quite sure it had made its home with us, then one day it disappeared. We found it later at a farm two miles away, but it wouldn't come back. It had become tired of us, just as it would become tired of the next farm.'

'Vet treated she-cats,' said a third gloomily, 'never live for long in the country. All the farm cats in the neighbourhood will descend upon her, corner her and kill her.'

Heaven knows why some people sadistically enjoy giving advice when it is too late for the advice to be accepted. We could do nothing now about Lama; and yet our informant continued to describe in detail the fate of one of his she-cats. 'Farm cats are real killers,' he added, 'when it comes to treated she-cats.'

'I don't believe a word of it,' I said, while Jeannie got up and went out of the room, 'and what a damn stupid thing to say. It can only worry us.'

There was meanwhile the question to be answered: where had Lama come from? We had to find out whether there was somebody unhappily looking for her . . . but where *could* she have come from?

There were two farms at the top of the lane on the way to the main road. Farm cats galore inhabited them. Lama ought to have come from there, but she hadn't. No one knew of a little black cat being lost. There was a farm a quarter of a mile further on towards Lamorna, and another the same distance in the other direction. No help from either of them. There were other farms within a radius of three miles or so, and here also we drew a blank. None of them had any cats which were lost, nor could they help us with information about mother cats who had disappeared at the moment of confinement. And in any case why should a mother cat disappear from the comfort of a house or a barn to have her kittens outside, in the midst of a hard winter? For if the vet was correct in his calculations, Lama was born in December.

My investigations had, of course, been pursued before Lama had been taken away to be treated. I had to admit, however, that they had been done in a hurry. A lip service investigation so-to-speak, and each time I had asked: 'Have you lost a little black cat?' I had prayed for the answer to be no. The source of my anxiety was romantic rather than practical. I might have found Lama's original home, and then been kindly told by the owner that we could keep her. But this would not have suited me at all. I wanted to combine the act of keeping her, with the maintenance of an illusion; and because she had arrived so mysteriously, I hoped that her past would also remain mysterious. An indulgence on my part. A desire to see the remark I had made, after Monty had died, come true. I was indeed like someone who was wanting to bend the facts to suit his wishful thinking.

Having failed to find any clues by my personal enquiries, I was for a short time content to believe that I could do no more.

'She's ours, Jeannie,' I said, after I had come back from the last farm, 'nobody knows anything about her.'

'She's a magical cat.'

'It's not as if we were in a town where she could have come from a hundred different homes in the neighbourhood. There's only a choice of nine or ten.'

'She may have travelled a long distance, I suppose.'

'How could she have survived the bitter weather?'

'She's such a *little* cat.'

'And why should she have travelled towards Minack, passing the farms on the way, then stayed round here?'

'She'd heard of the vacancy.'

'She took long enough to make up her mind once she got here. After all she hardly rushed to introduce herself.'

'That was feminine intuition,' said Jeannie, 'you'd have thrown her out if she'd forced herself on you.'

'Oh yes, I understand all that fanciful nonsense,' I said laughing, 'but she must have come from somewhere. I feel sure logically minded people would have a clear answer.'

'You don't *want* a clear answer,' replied Jeannie, 'so I wouldn't worry any more.'

I remained, however, uneasy. I am prepared to fool myself temporarily, prepared to make any situation coincide with my preconceived hopes, but fortunately I have a belated toughness which erodes my momentary satisfaction as soon as I am freed from the emotion which the situation has created. Hence over-enthusiasm soon cools into reappraisal or, conversely, indignation simmers into proper perspective. In this particular case the aftermath of my investigations was this unease. Somebody, somewhere must have known her when she was a kitten. It wasn't as if she was any old tabby. She was a beautiful little black cat which anyone would clearly remember. Even a farmer, with a horde of cats lodging among his farm buildings, would have noticed Lama.

Then suddenly I remembered the travelling fish salesman from Newlyn, and I wondered why I had not thought of him before. Here was a man who was ideally placed to solve the problem once and for all, a man who was known to every cat in the Land's End peninsula. He once told me that when his van drew up at a farmhouse he used to see cats racing across fields to join the group around him as he showed his wares to the farmer's wife. He was the cats' friend. Each day of the week he visited a different area, loading up at Newlyn market in the morning not only with fresh fish to sell but also with less favoured fish to give away. No wonder cats recognised his grey van. No wonder they remembered the day of the week on which he called. He was the Pied Piper of fish salesmen. He knew the cats who lived twenty miles and more away from Minack. He took a personal interest in them, and if he observed a regular was absent from the group around the open back door of his van, he would ask the farmer's wife for news. He was part of the stream of feline life in West Cornwall. Kittens were introduced to him by their mothers. Old cats, past hunting days, relied on him. No one was in a better position to tell us where Lama had come from.

I asked him to call, and we showed him Lama. He had never seen her before. A week went by, and as he travelled his daily round he made enquiries at every stop. Then I saw him again.

He had met no one who had lost a little black cat.

Where, then, had she come from? It was a long time before we learnt her secret.

9

WE NOW began to become acquainted with Lama. She was, as I have said, very small. She remained very small. In Monty's heyday when I put him on the potato weighing machine, the scales read eighteen and a half pounds. The same scales when I weighed Lama read seven and a half pounds.

She was the epitome of a chocolate box or a Christmas card cat. The allure of a cat is at its perfection when its head is in perfect proportion to its body, and when its tail has a character of its own. Lama's tail was like the handle of a cup, a firm curve demanding to be clasped and lifted. I developed, in fact, the trick which Lama permitted, whereby I clasped this handle of a tail so that in one movement I lifted posterior and back paws.

The paws were tiny, with black pigments. They were like little black powderpuffs and yet, when she was on the attack, they stabbed with the viciousness of needles.

She was black from the tip of her nose to the tip of her tail, except for a wisp of a white shirt. Monty had a white shirt which was so bold that you could see it in the dark before you caught sight of his figure. You had to look hard to see Lama's even in daylight, just a vague hint of white, a shadow against black. She also had a single white whisker. It was on the left as she stared at you; and Jeannie alleged it came and went according to the long distance prospects of the weather. Hence if the weather was going to be cold and wet and stormy, the whisker flourished; if a heat wave lay ahead, it wilted and dropped off. I do not vouch for this fanciful interpretation of the life of the whisker. I have intended to take notes, plot a weather chart, and draw a graph displaying the growth of the whisker week by week. I will do so one day. In the meantime the whisker blossoms for a month or two, looks incongruous against its lush black neighbours, then suddenly disappears.

'White whisker has gone,' one of us would say, as if we were mentioning the end of a cherry tree's blossom time. And we would also remark a little later, when we had been observant enough to notice it: 'White whisker is growing again.'

Lama was very soft to touch. She was, of course, so light when you held her in your arms that you felt there was no weight to carry, or if there was a weight you could describe it as being a parcel of swan's feathers. This gossamer quality was deceptive. Hold Lama against her co-operation and you felt her muscles stiffen into a ramrod; and as your hands clasped her you were uneasily aware that you held a small stick of dynamite. All claws and hisses. A pivot of intense fury in a small body. And if you were wise you would immediately disengage from this cat who had momentarily gone wild. And you would do it promptly.

Cat lovers, I have found, those all embracing lovers of every kind of cat, show great irritation when their love receives little response. A battle of wills ensues and it sometimes appears to me that the cat lover, the alleged cat lover, is a bit heartless. Vanity is wounded when purrs do not immediately operate. Tempers are even frayed if the cat concerned remains obstinately aloof. Cats, it seems, are expected to throw their arms around their human lovers with the same enthusiasm as the latter throw their arms around cats. And if they don't the lover's knot is often cut. One day, for instance, after many people had visited us, Lama had gone to bed first and settled comfortably, as far as she was concerned, a few inches below my pillow. I tried, like a contortionist, to get in between the sheets without disturbing her; and while I was twisting my way past her, Lama watching me with a baleful eye, I suddenly caught sight of a gap in her fur, just at one side of her spinal column. I looked at it in astonishment. One of the visitors had cut away a tuft about an inch square.

We never did find out how it happened.

Lama's eyes were oriental to look at, amber slits slanting upwards, and when strangers looked at her closely, they would say nine times out of ten: 'There's something strange about her. I can't quite place what it is.' Of course with her black eyelashes and the black background of her fur, the slanting amber eyes were accentuated. Yet there *was* something strange about her. She didn't look like any of the cats in the district. She resembled a half caste, in the terms of a human being, who was living in the western world.

I remember, in the beginning with us, how she had the most terrible nightmares. She would be curled up somewhere asleep when suddenly her whole little body would start shuddering, accompanied by gasping, whimpering cries, until the fear in the dream became so real that she woke up.

Nor did she know how to play, or how to knead. She did not, therefore, have the attributes of a normal kitten, and we had to help her to develop them. I am inclined to believe that kneading is a more subtle expression of pleasure than a purr. A purr is a boisterous acclamation in comparison. The knead, that gentle in and out movement of paws and claws, is a private demonstration of serene ecstasy; and it is, I feel, the surest sign of all that a cat is content. The conventional knead requires, of course, a cushion, or something soft and inviting like the counterpane of a bed; but the happiest knead of all to watch is a cat lying with lazy abandon on its side or its back, nothing for it to clasp, no object being used as a victim, just kneading. You see then the wonderful secret thoughts finding their way to expression. A cat in a private heaven.

The first game I tried to play with Lama was with a piece of string, dragging it temptingly in front of her. The gesture to her was incomprehensible. I tickled her with a pipe cleaner, I pretended my hand was a mouse by rustling it in a tuft of grass, I played all sorts of silly games without receiving the smallest reaction. She was above games. She was a Ninotchka. Life was deadly serious, and there was no time for humour. It was pathetic to watch her ignore any effort to entertain her, and depressing too.

'Isn't she *ever* going to play?' I said almost in despair after one particular patient attempt on my part.

'She will,' said Jeannie.

We had to wait a long time. The summer and autumn passed by, and it was not until a week before Christmas that the breakthrough took place. It was Shelagh's doing. Jane used to go back across the fields to her cottage for lunch but Shelagh, living further away, brought sandwiches. She used to sit eating them in the flower house, and she had two companions who often shared them with her, and who fortunately never met. One was a mouse who sat on her knee, the other was Lama.

We were particularly rushed at that time bunching freesia for the Christmas market; and we used raffia to tie the stems of the bunches. The raffia comes to us tied together at one end, but the other end is a bush of dried grasses. These grasses are cut off at the length required for the bunches.

The raffia was hanging from a nail above the packing bench, and Lama was on this bench. Shelagh pushed a pencil through the bush so that the tip appeared mysteriously a few inches from Lama's face. A paw was doubtfully raised.

Then the paw tried to attack the tip, treating it as if it were a red hot poker. Violent interest was aroused. Inhibitions disappeared. And by the time Shelagh's sandwiches had been consumed, the truth had dawned on Lama. They were playing a game.

It was a pleasant curtain for Christmas.

10

'MERRY CHRISTMAS!'

I was holding Lama in my arms and between her paws
was a parcel for Jeannie.

'Merry Christmas!'

The parcel was a deceptively large parcel. There was a
great amount of unnecessary packing. An elaborate intention to prolong the discovery of Lama's first Christmas
present. A small brooch. And attached to it was a verse I
had made up.

'*What* a lovely brooch!' said Jeannie. And I gave her
Lama, and Lama then fell on the wrapping paper spread on
the bed; and she obviously wondered what all the fuss was
about.

Her first Christmas at Minack was Angus's second. In
Monty's time, when Jeannie's mother was joining us, Angus
spent the period of festivities in kennels. There was the
usual heart-searching before he was sent off to his lodgings,
and periodically during her stay Jeannie's mother would
inevitably ruminate: 'I wonder how Angus is getting on?'

But this Christmas, against my better judgment, Angus
was invited, and the first confrontation between him and
Lama took place on Christmas Eve. I had depressingly
awaited the outcome. Still vivid in my mind was that
terrible encounter between Monty and Judy, and the explosion seemed ready to be repeated. Lama had had nine months
on her own. No dog had visited us. How would she cope

48

with a dog sharing the three rooms of the cottage? I was ready for the worst.

It is my nature to prepare for the worst. I feel by so doing that I leave a large margin of potential happiness in any problem in which I am involved, since the result can never be quite as bad as I expected. Hence, to whatever extent I am rebuffed, I am also relieved.

At that moment when I carried Lama to Jeannie, the confrontation had, of course, already taken place.

Jeannie had met them at Penzance station. They had travelled on the Cornish Riviera and Angus had spent the journey in the compartment. I have myself in the past felt resentful when a dog has been brought into my compartment. I have rustled my newspaper in an exaggerated fashion in order to display my annoyance. I have glared at the innocent creature. I have even changed to another compartment. But I always noticed that the dog's owner was quite unperturbed. Angus was Jeannie's mother's only companion in London and she too was unperturbed. 'Everybody loved him on the train,' she thus said as she walked with Jeannie down the platform, 'he's such a good little dog.'

And this was true. He did not have the pugnacity of a Judy, or of some Scotties. He was friendly without being obsequious. He did not yap unnecessarily. True he pulled hard when on his lead, and so Jeannie was sometimes concerned that he was too strong for her mother. Yet who can blame a dog for a small vice like that when he lives his life in a London flat, his regular walks are on pavements, and even in a park he cannot run at random? No wonder he revelled in his visits to Minack.

I watched the Land Rover splash through Monty's Leap and come up the last stretch of the lane past the stables, then round the steep piece to the right, and pull up in front of the window through which I was watching. The new coat, the new hat. I saw in the instant of watching that here again

I was witnessing the wish to please. Not to be thought casual. An effort made, much thought before the choice was finally decided upon. Another Christmas, and yet seemingly no gap since the last one. Gaily wrapped parcels in the two suitcases in the well of the Land Rover. Just the same as it always has been. Only the wink of an eyelid to note the passing of time.

I have never looked upon time as a hill, hiding the past on its other side. Time to me is a plain, so that if the circumstances are right, if the associations are in union, the past can be seen like a fire; and the feelings repeated, recognised again after being forgotten, the old story of Citizen Kane remembering his beginning, of Marcel Proust's *madeleine*, of all our minds when we are not controlled by doctrine. You touch the past as if it were the present. You meet yourself again as a ten-year-old at a moment of anguish or great joy, you are there again at first love; nothing has changed, you are as you always have been.

And so it was when Angus came into the room and Lama was lying Trafalgar-lionwise beneath my desk. Sixteen years ago when Monty was introduced to Judy. A heaving of time and yet to me I was living again the same moment. I had the same tenseness, the same belief that a decision had been made at the expense of sanity. An explosion was about to detonate, either the cat or the dog would be hurt, the Christmas would be spoilt before it had begun, an armed camp would be set up as at St Albans those years ago; and, as then, I was aware that I was impotently watching.

It was at this point the similarity ended. My role of 'I told you so' never matured. There I was, the figure of doom, being forced to smile. I am resilient in such matters and when I am proved wrong, I do not sulk. I appear gay, a gaiety which is genuine enough though others might take it as a pretence. Here I stood then, in the middle of the room, welcoming my mother-in-law in peace, instead of amid the cat and dog fight I had foretold. I was beaming with relief. I was thankful that the spirit of Christmas was apparently assured.

For what had happened was this. Angus came rollicking into the room, stumpy tail wagging, rushed up to me putting his nose to my shoes, nibbling the toe-caps, grinning, making a gurgling noise, and showing such total signs of delight that he was back in the country again, that it was crystal clear that he was in no mood for argument. Thus it all depended on Lama.

She was, as I have said, beneath my desk. And while I was being flattered by the attentions of Angus, out of the corner of my eye I was observing her. It was as if I were looking at a child who was assessing a child visitor. The aloof stare hiding intense interest. The mysterious process at work detailed to judge the extent of competition. An apparent nonchalance which deceived no one who knew her. And yet pervading her manner there was the suggestion she was prepared to be friends on reasonable conditions. Such conditions I guessed, revolved round Jeannie and me. During Angus's stay we had to make a quite exceptional fuss of her. There must not be a shadow of suspicion that she had been surplanted as queen of the household. With no difficulty we accepted these conditions. Angus could flounder in happiness, while Lama was caressed. It was a satisfactory compromise.

The following day was Christmas Eve, and in the evening there had been the customary busy gathering of presents, names scribbled on holly edged cards, separate little groups of parcels placed side by side under the Christmas tree. All day Angus and Lama had tolerated each other. Angus fussed in and out of the cottage, rushing up and down the path outside, and when we took him for a walk he scadaddled across the fields, stumpy tail wagging, a joyous little dog on holiday. Lama, on the other hand, maintained a distant air. *She* did not have to behave with vulgar abandon. *She* was the châtelaine of the cottage; this dog, however amiable he might be, was an interloper. She wouldn't be rude, but there was no need to behave as if she *liked* his presence. You could see he was pampered and that he knew all about Christmasses. This was her first. The first in the company of human beings who were so clearly anxious to pay court to her. It was advisable for her to remain distant in any case. It was a defence. How could she know how to behave?

Jeannie and her mother, as part of the game of Christmas, filled a stocking each for Angus and Lama. A packet of dog biscuits and a tin of meat for Angus and little presents of only sentimental importance; and a packet of Felix for Lama and a toy mouse, and one or two other things which Jeannie put in and were really meant for me. But, as a special gesture towards thé occasion, Jeannie had cooked in advance the turkey giblets and, wrapped in grease proof paper, she had shared them between the two stockings. Each stocking, a gauze imitation of a stocking, was hung by a drawing pin at one end of the bookcase.

Early on Christmas morning Jeannie and I were awakened by a crackling, crunching sound. Not noisy. Just a reminder as to what happens when a mouse is consumed.

Our fault, of course. Lama had found the giblets.

TWO YEARS LATER

1

'LAMA'S AT the window.'

'I saw.'

'Let her in. I'm peeling the potatoes.'

'I've just let her out.'

'Mrs In and Out as Tannie would say. Go on . . . '

Tannie was my aunt who was over eighty years old, and she came down once a year from London for a holiday at Minack. At some other time of the year she would fly by night-flight to some corner of Europe for a holiday, and we would receive pithy postcards from places well off the tourist's map. She was young in spirit. She was wonderfully interested in modern trends of art, literature, and politics, but she was never swayed into over-valuing them by the hysteria of any small influential group. She judged every new fashion on its merits.

She was part of the world I was brought up in as a child which was solidly anti-cat. I am quite sure she would never under any circumstances have possessed a cat of her own, for cats all her life had been distasteful beasts; but she was fair about Lama. She thought her very pretty. She went further by saying that Lama had a style about her, a symmetry of limbs and body, equivalent to that of a thoroughbred racehorse. Such a comparison may sound extravagant; but my aunt believed that quality had a common denominator. It might be the swing of a golfer, a small part in a play, always Jane Austen, a final at Wimbledon, a concert at the Festival Hall, or the way somebody polished the silver; all these things had a standard in her mind which, if fulfilled, provided pure pleasure.

I got up and opened the door. Lama had been sitting on the window ledge so that she had only to jump down on the stone paving outside the cottage and then come in through the porch. She hesitated, peering below her.

'Boris is waiting to pinch her tail,' I said to Jeannie.

Boris had come to Minack after a boy friend of Jane's had offered him to her for dinner. He was a magnificent Muscovy drake, a large white bird the size of a goose, with dark green feathers on his back, a pink beak with a red bobble, huge yellow webbed feet, intelligent eyes, and the habit of raising the crest of feathers on his head when annoyed. The boy friend had arrived at Jane's cottage with Boris in a sack. He was, so Jane told me later, very proud of his gift, confident that it was an imaginative way of wooing her. But he could not have known Jane very well. She burst into angry tears, accused the young man of great cruelty, rescued Boris from the sack, and carried him upstairs. And when Jane came to work across the fields she was carrying Boris in her arms. She also brought a message from her mother: Boris, her mother thought reasonably enough, was too much of a handful to be kept in a bedroom. Would we give him a home? And of course we did.

Boris had arrived fifteen months ago, Lama three months before that; and so they had grown acclimatised to Minack together, and while doing so had watched each other closely. Their relationship for a long time was warfare without battle; and I sometimes interpreted their behaviour towards each other as being an example of old fashioned class consciousness. Boris considered himself as good as Lama, and he preened himself and strutted about sure he was a noble bird: but why should he live in an old chicken house, have to wait in the morning for the door to be opened, while *she* enjoyed a pampered life indoors? The trouble was that

Lama encouraged him to think in this way. She would walk past him with a nonchalant, provocative lilt, a young lady sure of her elegance and financial security; and this air of subtle superiority provoked Boris with his splendid though heavy appearance into floundering, into being enraged like a blindfolded giant, into clumsily weaving his head of raised feathers to and fro towards Lama as she passed him, vulgarly hissing meanwhile, and leaving the impression after Lama had serenely gone by, that he was cursing himself for having fallen into her trap; and had attacked instead of remaining loftily silent.

Boris, therefore, was sometimes a little distressed. He believed himself placed at a disadvantage. He was basically farmyard, Lama was a creature of soft cushions. Why should birth be so unfair? His revenge was to harry her, to make her beware of his presence, to keep her always in doubt whether his fierce appearance was genuine or show; and Lama countered with an upturned nose as she passed him. Indeed she was never seriously concerned by his behaviour, for instinct told her he was feigning. And in any case Lama, since her arrival from the wild, had clearly developed the belief that harm would never threaten her. She was a cat in heaven, and the world was always kind. Thus her mood towards Boris, appearing sometimes to be haughty, was that of indifference. His hisses, to her way of thinking, were as empty in content as the last gasp of a soda water siphon.

Nevertheless her confidence occasionally resulted in over-confidence, and for a while afterwards she would treat him with greater respect. There was a period, for instance, when they each took the same liking to a small empty greenhouse we have near the cottage. A pleasant sun parlour for them both.

'Lama and Boris are having coffee together,' Jeannie would say ridiculously. Boris near the open door, Lama on a sack in the centre. It was here that I witnessed one of Boris's rare victories.

Lama, dozy in the warmth, lulled into off-guard contentment, had turned on her back, four tiny paws at different angles in the air, an inviting black silk tummy, eyes shut, blissful thoughts; and suddenly into this sweet oblivion Boris decided to advance.

Boris was heavy enough to make a sound on gravel like a person walking on the path. I have often heard the noise of his webbed feet, and been deceived, and cried out to Jeannie: 'Somebody's coming!' But it was only Boris plodding up the path, wanting a piece of Jeannie's homemade bread, or just needing our company and feeling he would achieve it by sentry-going on the soil and the plants of the small garden outside the door. But on this occasion he walked with stealth. A muscovy drake's tip toe. His beak had a target.

I arrived by chance at the greenhouse at the instant of strike. The supple softness of Lama was hopelessly vulnerable. There she lay lost in her dreams, the careless abandon of a happy cat, a nymph at the mercy of the hypnotic powers of the sun; and I suddenly saw Boris a split second away from making his dab.

It was only a dab. I saw for myself there was nothing vicious in its intent. His head, feathers tufted, moved towards her centre, backwards and forwards, nearer and nearer, like the uncertain movements of an old fashioned movie; and it only needed one dab from his beak which hit the middle of her tummy, for Lama to leap to her feet, like a cornered cowboy drawing pistols in a flash and firing them at the sudden enemy. Only in her case the weapons were fur flushed upright, arched back, a growl, and claws like daggers.

Boris gloried in his triumph. He wagged his tail feathers fussily in delight. He had made a fool of her. He stood a few feet away, opened up his huge wings and flapped them noisily and with such vigour that the draught put up a little eddy of dust and scurried a leaf across the ground of the greenhouse. His was a demonstration of how to say boo to the boss. Or to an acquaintance with superior airs. A little cunning, a little finesse, a second of impetuous courage, and the moral victory is won. No question of pursuing the joke any further. Let her simmer in vanity-wounded fury. He would stump off. He had no wish for a brawl. He would leave her to ruminate upon her indignity. And I watched him plod away through the doorway, a cumbersome, happy drake, pad, pad, pad, until he reached the camellia bush opposite the packing shed; and which, for the time being, was his favourite resting place. He fluffed his feathers, and settled down to wait. How would she behave when next she saw him?

I observed, after the attack, how Lama concurred with Paul Gallico's cat comment: 'When in doubt, wash!' Lama washed in an exaggerated, busy fashion as if panic had seized her because the Queen was paying a visit, and her only dress was suddenly dirty. Lick, lick, lick, the vigorous action was aimed to cover up her enormous embarrassment. She had been caught napping. The ponderous yokel had nipped her. And her confusion, her reaction to the insult, the flash of fear in being so suddenly awoken, had been witnessed. No one, certainly not a cat, likes to be seen to be foolish. She was suffering the penalty of accepting civilisation. In the old days she could react to danger, real or apparent, with all the flamboyance of someone on the lone trail; and no one would know if sometimes the panic was misplaced. But this role she had chosen, this acceptance of the lush life, demanded that she could be laughed at if the situation deserved it. Those who are alone, anonymous in a big city or adventurous in the wild, can keep their secrets. Compromise, become dependent on others, be gregarious or conventional, and the door opens on the bathroom. The grievous moments become raw instead of hidden, and there is no longer the opportunity to slide away to nurse them in private peace. The hounds have seen and they are baying.

Lama washed. And when she realised that her deceptive effort was making me smile, she got up and went over to one of the wooden trestles we had in the greenhouse, and elaborately began using it as a scratching board. All she was doing was giving herself time to think, to recover her composure and to work out her next move.

And as it happens her next move was predictable. She stopped her clawing, sauntered apparently unconcernedly out of the greenhouse, then suddenly went on the alert.

She was pretending she had heard a mouse in the grass.

2

ONE EARLY afternoon that winter, not long before Christmas, we lost Lama down a badger hole. She had gone down badger holes before, indeed she was fascinated by badger holes, and so we ought to have learnt our lesson. We hadn't, thus there came a moment when we thought we would never see her again.

Jeannie and I had gone on a stroll round our daffodil meadows, and Lama had chosen to accompany us. I have never found it a particularly peaceful experience taking Lama for a walk. There are so many delays. There I am walking happily along, and suddenly I am told by piercing jungle miaows that I am going too fast. I am not. I am deliberately mooching so as not to rush her, and yet for some reason of her own, just to assert her authority perhaps, she bellows her protest; and I have to stop. She then trots fast towards me, takes no notice when she reaches me, and scampers quickly ahead. Then she waits for me to catch up with her, waits behind after I have done so, and performs the same rigmarole all over again. Sick humour on her part. For she makes her miaows so heartrending that I am forced to believe she is really distressed. I am a fool to do so.

The meadows Jeannie and I were walking among were those we called the Far Meadows. They were beneath an old carn, ancient meadows which probably had been used for one crop or another for centuries. A great place for adders, it was said. Never put your coat down on the ground, we had been warned. A man once did so, picked up the jacket at the end of his day's work, put his arm down a sleeve; and the adder nipped him. That's where the story ends. No news as to what happened to the man.

It is joyous to look at the meadows when the green sheaves of the daffodils are first bursting the soil. Bed upon bed of them, each brimming with hope for us who depend upon them for our livelihood. And part of the fun, sometimes the disappointment, of the stroll is for me to bend down, and to pinch with my fingers the collar of the bulbs. Green leaves may be growing but this does not mean that flowers will follow; and you learn to feel whether or not a bud is on the way, and if you have pinched a number of them, spaced here and there in different beds, you come to know long before the daffodil harvest begins whether or not it is going to be successful.

There are words of mine still floating on Minack cliffs. Contradictory words. Some belong to one season, some to another.

'Jeannie! There are no buds at all. None at all. It's going to be a terrible season.'

'Let's not be over confident . . . but I believe there are more buds this year than I've ever known before.'

'I'm nervous, Jeannie. There seem to be plenty of Obs, but the Mags seem terribly light.'

Jeannie and I have so many times looked at the meadows; and seen superimposed upon them our bank statement.

That year was the last in which we grew flowers specially for our Cornish posies. I think of all the flowers we have ever grown those which ended up mixed in the posies were our favourites. For the posies were so exquisitely arranged by Jeannie, Jane and Shelagh that each bloom therein was a jewel, different from its neighbour; and each one, though we began sending them away to market in November and continued to do so throughout the winter, had the scent of spring. We had forget-me-nots in a greenhouse, long rows of orange marigolds in a field near the wood, freesias in another greenhouse, polyanthus, brightly coloured anemones, Beauty of Nice winter flowering stocks, and seldom less than an acre of wallflowers. Wallflowers were the mainstay of the posies, giving them bulk and the background of rich dark green leaves and the scented petals of blood red Vulcan and Yellow Phoenix and Primrose. And if you had been there after the three of them had been bunching all day, and saw on the shelves row upon row of the posies, each in a jam jar of water, close together, filling the packing shed with spring, a kaleidoscope of colour, then you would have said to yourself as we have done so many times: this is the sight to make the cynic happy.

I remember, or perhaps I comfort myself by remembering, that once upon a time, people had the luxury of doing a job they enjoyed, took pride in its craftsmanship, and earned enough to cover their expenses. We found with our posies that this did not occur. When we first sent them to market our salesman told us they were the sensation of Covent Garden, and that he could take as many as we could send. CORNISH POSIES from TANGYE, ST BURYAN, were asked for by every important flower shop in London. And so we expanded, and grew more of all the necessary flowers, and worked harder; for the act of work was not just the task of bunching them, of packing them which Jeannie did so beautifully, but there was also the months and months of caring for the plants. And having cared for them, there was the picking; and after the picking there was the stripping of the leaves from the wallflowers, the forget-me-nots, the marigolds, and the stock, all these tasks took many, many hours of working time. Yet, as seasons went by, so did the prices for our posies become lower; and then one day our eyes were opened when someone told us what had happened. The flower shops had found it cheaper to make up posies on the premises. They bought the various flowers separately on the market, then fashioned the CORNISH POSIES themselves.

We had Obvallaris in the Far Meadows, and these too went into the posies during their flowering time. Obvallaris; such a dull, ugly name, hiding the exquisite little daffodils which look like miniature King Alfreds. They were ideal for the posies; but sent away in bunches on their own they could not compete in the market with the fashionable varieties. There were five of these small meadows of Obvallaris, and one of Scilly Whites; and they all peered downwards towards the sea. Heaven knows how long the Scilly Whites had lain in that meadow, thirty or forty years perhaps, but they still bloomed their white clusters of flowers, reaching you with scent that rejoices with hope. Of course Scilly Whites are early flowering and as the name obviously suggests, it is the Isles of Scilly which grows them earliest and best. Sometimes we ourselves had them in bloom before Christmas but on this occasion, this occasion when Lama was accompanying us on our walk, the season was a late one; there was no chance of a stem scenting the cottage at Christmas.

All around these meadows was uncouth country of bracken and boulders, of flamboyant grasses and ominous brambles, of quickthorn and sharply pricking gorse, of the sense of the constant fall to the massive rocks and sea below; all these things wrapped me, when I stood among them, with the knowledge that here was reality. For here too were the trampled paths of the foxes and badgers; and if you stand on one of those paths, then realise that they have been used for centuries, you are a tough unimaginative soul if you do not feel humbled.

It seemed that Lama knew these paths in the Far Meadows intimately. She scampered up the beaten, foot wide tracks as if they were giving her a welcome. She crouched on the lip of a stone hedge where a track led from one meadow to another, and when I approached she raced away again. She seemed to be at home. There were no loud protesting miaows as occurred when we took her on an ordinary walk. She behaved as if she had gone wild again.

There was a track which led across the Scilly White meadow, well trodden, the green spears of the Scilly Whites bent and bruised, stunted and curling, no time for them to become upright before the pads of badgers crushed them. In this age when the cool calculations of the accountant advise the removal of sentiment from any business, the badgers on our cliffs should have been removed. They do not respect our daffodils. They dig among them if they so desire. If we plant them on a piece of ground across which for centuries they have been accustomed to plod, the gesture of man will not stop them from continuing to plod. It's their land, not ours. We are the interlopers. And in the end the damage they do does not amount to much. But enough, perhaps, for the apostles of logic to argue that it is illogical to allow them to continue to roam these glorious, secret, untamed cliffs where we try to earn a living.

Suddenly Lama darted along this track, then disappeared into the cavern of undergrowth at the other end of the meadow.

'Lama!' called Jeannie, 'where are you going?'

I myself knew very well.

'Lama!' I shouted, 'come back!'

There was a splendid badger sett among the undergrowth into which Lama had disappeared, and the under-growth mainly consisted of a forest of blackthorn. Have you ever crawled on the ground where blackthorn grows? All the growth of the blackthorn is at the top of its prickly wooden stem, and so when badgers make their home among blackthorn, their paths criss cross below as they do in the open. They did here, and I was soon to sample them.

'There's not a sign of her.'

I had gone down on my knees and was staring into the gloom, and when my eyes became accustomed to it, I noticed the scattering of dried twigs and clumps of bracken which were the old discarded bedding of the badgers. There it all was on well pounded paths, slimy soil that never saw the light, pointing to journeys over the years. I sensed I was about to be exasperated. I also sensed that I was the witness of shadows. If I were about to be infuriated by a cat, I was also rewarded by the feeling of continuity in life.

'I can tell you where she's gone,' I said.

'Where?'

'Down the largest badger hole I've ever seen.'

This was not quite true. I had seen this hole before. It was one of the group of the sett which covered several hundred square yards of the cliff. And Jeannie had always said that this sett was one of the most desirable badger residences in the country. Well covered; glorious views of the sea and immune, it seemed, to human interference.

'Lama!'

The note in my voice had become sharper. It was two o'clock in the afternoon, and we had other things to do than to shout for Lama.

'Lama!'

This time it was Jeannie. She too had gone down on to her knees; and there were the two of us, side by side, our backs to the Scilly Whites, growing irritable, at the mercy of a cat in a hole.

'You had better go down into it,' said Jeannie.

'I can't go into the hole!'

'You can get into the undergrowth and put your hand down the hole. She's probably just inside.'

The hole was only a few feet away but to get there I had to wriggle along the badger path, umbrella of blackthorn above me hiding the light, flat on my tummy, the musk scent of badgers around me; then I reached the entrance, and at

66

the top of my voice I shouted again: 'Lama!'

The maddening thing about a situation like this can be the side irritations it produces. Hence Jeannie and I, irritated by Lama, began to be irritated by each other. I heard her voice behind me.

'Don't shout!' she said, 'you'll wake up the badgers and they'll be after her.'

'Stuff and nonsense,' I said, my mouth inches from the clammy soil. Then I added mercilessly: 'They've probably eaten her already.'

There was, needless to say, no response from Lama. Nor when I embraced the entrance, then stretched my arm at its full length down the hole, did my fingers touch any soft fur. Lama had disappeared.

I wriggled my way back to the Scilly Whites and said to Jeannie it would be a good idea if she took my place; and I would keep silent, and she could try the effects of her own dulcet tones. I watched her, in blue denims, snake her way to the entrance.

'Lama!' I then heard, whispered, quite different from my own barrack square tone. 'Lama! Come on . . . we're waiting for you.'

'Like hell we are,' I murmured to myself; and I anticipated that Jeannie would blame her own failure to tempt response on my own brave shouts of 'Lama!'

But I was quite wrong. She had also become angry with the cat. She waited for a few moments in the undergrowth, then backed herself out.

'The bread has to go in the oven. I must get back to the cottage.'

I watched her go up the path past the carn, then left to myself I waited a few minutes until I guessed she was well out of earshot; then I let go. And a series of: 'LAMA!' echoed round the cliffs.

I was quite aware that I had lost my temper; and my

reason for doing so had its depths in my bringing-up antipathy to cats. They were too independent, too selfish, too stupid . . . . all these things I had been told about them. These views were inbred in me. I had been captured by Monty because he was an anchor at a critical time; but what did Lama mean to me? An hour had gone by, two hours . . . the rocks below were passing into shadow, etched by the foam; and we were wasting our time courting a cat; a wild, ungrateful cat, symbol of selfish individualism, and yet so dependent upon us that it would be miserable if we were not there to obey its commands. I was fed up with looking for it. If it were devoured by a mad badger or a hungry fox . . . well, it didn't matter as far as I was concerned. I was going.

I passed Jeannie on my way back to the cottage. The bread, safely baked, she was returning with tempting morsels in a bag. Jeannie, the cat lover, had complete faith in bribery. It was now dark, and she carried a torch.

'So you're leaving Lama?'

'What else can I do? I've shouted myself hoarse.'

'The last five per cent. That's what counts.'

'Oh hell,' I said, 'don't sound so demanding. I've been on my hands and knees after that damned cat for hours, I don't care a damn if I never see it again.'

'I'll go on my own.'

'Yes, you do.' And I pounded away from her into the darkness.

I got back to the cottage, picked up a newspaper and angrily began to read it. The cat had put me in the wrong. The story had started so innocently, just a walk with no other intention except to relax. And now hours later it had ended up with friction between Jeannie and me. Perhaps I ought to go and have another look. I rustled the paper noisily. Yes, perhaps I *had* to have another look.

At that particular moment the cottage door opened.

Jeannie came in and in her arms was Lama.

'I only had to call her,' she said in the tone of victory, 'and she came to me.'

'Yes, yes,' I said quickly though quietly, 'just shows your influence.' Then I added vehemently: 'But it was the food that got it out. Not you!'

'That's where you're wrong.'

'Why?'

'Lama was sitting at the exact spot where you had been shouting.'

3

'DO YOU know,' said Shelagh, bunching posies in the flower house, 'that it is . . .'

'Yes, yes, I know, Shelagh. It is eight days to Christmas.'

'Nine.'

'All right, nine,' I said.

'One could say, of course,' Shelagh went on, smiling at the flowers she held in her hand, 'that as we are half way through the morning, today doesn't count. Then you would be right. Only eight days to Christmas.'

'Agreed. Eight days.'

Shelagh began this game as soon as a Christmas was over. And it went on throughout the year. Three hundred days, two hundred days, thirty, five . . . The figure would be brought out with a shy smile at a dull moment. And the rest of us, Jane, myself and Jeannie would bellow in mock horror: 'Oh, Shelagh, don't remind us that the year is going so fast!' Simple jokes can be funny ones when the tempo is flower bunching.

Jeannie's mother and Angus were coming again. Jeannie's mother was like Shelagh; long before the rest of us were thinking of Christmas she would be writing kind letters and asking: 'What would Derek like?' Or to me: 'What would Jean like?' Here was an example of prolonging the pleasure of giving. No last minute gesture or salving of conscience. No extravagance to hide the fact that the receiver had been forgotten. This was a campaign, a considered assessment of hints given and observations made; and ending with all the anxiety that accompanies the edge of victory. Do you like it? Are you sure you like it? And if momentarily you are taken aback, surprised by the way your desires are interpreted by others, the force of goodwill behind the giving stirs you to thank. Wonderful! Fabulous! And sometimes you worry later whether the enthusiasm sounded empty.

One can be tedious about Christmas. One can, in fact, be so tedious that it becomes a bore. In this enlightened gimmick age, it is tedious to accept the idea that there can be one day in the year for which centuries demand goodwill; and so the excuse is made that it is too commercialised. That is true, of course. It is hopelessly commercialised. And yet this is still no reason to treat Christmas as an anachronism. For it will always be the time of old fashioned kindness, of evidence of truth, of pure unselfishness and, quite often, of unexpected exultation. And so with these qualities as its armour, there is no cause for anyone to consider Christmas as a bore. It demands an effort. That's all.

My own effort has been at its frailest when I have been anticipating Christmas. On this occasion, for instance, I was irked by the prospect of what happens when someone stays at Minack. In spring and summer the close quarters are unimportant because of the season. In winter, at Christmas, there is an inclination for everyone to be on top of each other; and that only means Jeannie and me, and the guest. The guest room, the converted chicken house, is between the sitting room and the bathroom, and with no communication, as a result, with our bedroom. Hence my toothpaste, my razor and my sponge, lodge for the duration of a visit in congested quarters around the kitchen sink. My clothes too, are unobtainable. I do not know where my shoes have been hidden. I yell for socks. I find myself circulating in our tiny bedroom trying to dress, trying to undress. It has been the anticipation of these minor inconveniences that

71

have demanded the effort on my part. They have loomed far larger than reality. The cold winds and early falling darkness magnify the effort I have to make.

A cat, one can well argue, has no right at all to object to momentary dislocation of its habits. Lama, of course, could not worry herself unnecessarily beforehand in the way that I did. She treated the situation as it came; and often she has caused Jeannie and myself much embarrassment by her rudeness. If, for instance, it is beyond her usual bedtime she will stamp up and down in front of the offending visitor as he sits on the sofa discoursing on some matter of great interest; and although the effect on the visitor may be nil, it results in Jeannie and I looking at each other, half laughing, and making us lose the thread of the discussion.

Lama was, of course, now acclimatised to Angus. There was no special friendship but, since the first Christmas, there had been other visits; and a toleration towards each other had been achieved. Lama clearly would much prefer his absence but, once he had arrived and was clearly at Minack to stay for a while, the truth had better be faced. She would not gain anything by attack.

There was, however, to be another visitor this Christmas; and I myself was apprehensive about this visitor. Jeannie, because she has always been bolder than me, pooh-poohed the idea that any risks were going to be taken. And although I was ready to agree with her, I remained irritated that even the prospect of a risk should have to exist at a time when minds should be at ease. The visitor was to be an Alsatian.

Tara, however, was a very old Alsatian. She belonged to my cousin Carol and he had a house at Nanquidno near the old mining town of St Just, five miles from Minack. I had been with him when he first had seen the house, and seldom could a possible new home have been first seen under gloomier circumstances. A thick fog blew up the valley from

72

the sea, so thick that I could not see the pond which featured in the garden in front of the house. Nor see the solid chimneys prodding from the roof. And a wall I saw looming in the greyness proved later to be a high hedge. It was no day to choose a house. No day even to sense its possibilities. My cousin Carol, however, thought otherwise. His Cornish ancestry provided him with the instinct that here was the home of his dreams. 'This is it, Tara old girl,' I heard him say, barely twenty minutes after arriving there, 'this is going to be our home.' He was a bachelor with a flat in London, and it took him a long time to break away from his London life; and, alone, he was now about to spend his first Christmas in Cornwall.

'You must come for Christmas dinner!' said Jeannie, 'come any day, any time, over the holiday!'

'What about Tara?'

'She too, of course,' said Jeannie, before I had time to interrupt.

Tara, when I first knew her, was a creature of splendour even in the midst of her breed. Her black marks against the silver sand of her coat, the magnificent head, the glorious way she stood when alert, with ears pricked and intelligent eyes staring at the mystery; all these qualities shone from her, sharing the common denominator of all things with fine breeding. And she was placid, too, and there was never any question of her becoming over excited in moments of stress. She was devoted to Carol, and when one thought of him, one also thought of Tara.

But now she was old. She was like a woman renowned once for her great beauty. The splendour was still to be observed, but it was obscured by a lack of lustre, a heaviness, a slow and jerky way of moving, eyes that were dull, all the sad accoutrements of age. She was, too, an invalid, and Carol was the permanent nurse. I am certain many people must have considered it ludicrous the way he looked after her. Special pills, special diet, all the inconveniences of semi-illness. And yet it was obvious to anyone that both of them were content.

It was, as it happens, Carol's nature to look after other people. He had had, all his life, the opportunity and the time to be kind in a practical fashion, one of those old fashioned Samaritans who put themselves to great inconvenience in order to give pleasure to others. He was small and rotund and bouncy; and although when I was a child he was a grown man, he now appeared to be ageless. He set out to be kind and corralled happiness around him. Only the mean minded could dislike him. He was humorous, but the humour was often derived from his vagueness. He could never, for instance, remember people's names. He would invite a few friends to his house, then flounder in confusion as he tried to introduce them to each other. A comical sight, but his charm easily overcame any embarrassment. He enjoyed life.

My concern, my reservation about Tara coming for Christmas, was due partly to her condition; a selfish reaction on my part that too much fuss might have to be made of her. And this was allied to my doubts as to how Lama and Angus might behave. It was going to be crowded in the cottage. Tara might possess a placid nature when she was treated like a queen on her own, but she might object to sharing the attention with a cat and a Scottie. One snap and there would be bedlam. And it all seemed so unfair on Lama. Her good manners would be tested to the utmost. No cat could be expected to *enjoy* entertaining a Scottie and an Alsation; and so I think she had every right to complain that we were taking her good nature for granted. After all, two years ago she had been a savage; and so wasn't it possible that the turmoil within her could be dormant, quelled for the present by the congenial circumstances in which she lived? Thus, if she were provoked, if she were annoyed by

74

the invasion of strangers, there might be every justification for her to say to herself: 'I'm off!'

In the afternoon, the day before Christmas Eve, Lama arranged herself on my lap. Up to that moment I had been busy. I had promised Jeannie, for instance, to clear my desk, and there were other tasks on my schedule. Then Lama jumped up after I, in a moment of laziness, had sat down on the sofa to glance at the paper; only for a second to glance at the headlines, no intention to avoid my responsibilities. But there on my knees was Lama.

She began to purr. It was not one of those ordinary purrs which one must admit are two a penny in any normal cat-happy circumstances. It was a roar. A glorious anthem praising to the heavens that she was the favoured one to live alone with us inside the cottage at Minack. It was a great burst of Christmas wishes. An expression of innocent delight that the three of us were together. And as I listened to her, drawing a finger up and down her black silky back, guilty about the things I should be doing but hypnotically relaxed by the sound of her, I heard a car draw up outside; then footsteps coming to the door.

It is always a challenge if duty demands that you should remove a contented cat from your lap. Insensitive people throw them to the floor without more ado. Others pray it will make its decision on its own. I heard the knock, thankfully saw Lama leap away from me, got up and went to open the door.

It was Mr Murley of Lamorna Post Office. Our letters came from St Buryan. Our telegrams from Lamorna. And he gave me one:

'May I spend Christmas with you unless family gathering. Jack.'

I hadn't seen him in years. I thought he was in America.

4

JACKIE BROADBENT was a legendary figure in the world of newspaper men. He was legendary partly because of his professionalism, but also as a result of his loyalty to his friends. In a world where daggers are perpetually being sharpened, he risked his own career time and again by supporting an out of favour colleague. It was, therefore, a question of the fates mocking him that he should himself have been prematurely retired.

He was a lovable, eccentric character who was frequently the despair of his friends because he would pursue routes which had no end. He was an idealist; and if his heart warmed towards someone or if ethics were at stake, he became a rock in their defence. He was shrewd. His political predictions, both home and international, were often dismissed at the time as too fanciful; and yet the years have proved their accuracy. He was endearingly generous in his hospitality. When my mother presented Jeannie at Court, he rang me up a few days before and said he guessed we would want to celebrate when it was all over; and as his flat was a short distance from the Palace, he would like to give us a party. He greeted my mother ebulliently: 'A special magnum of Bollinger for you, ma'am,' ladies of all ages were addressed as ma'am, 'in honour of you presenting the prettiest girl of them all at Court today!' And for Jeannie he had a bouquet of pink roses.

He had a habit of telephoning his friends and pretending

to be someone else. He was usually acute enough to choose a name that was in the mind of the person he was telephoning. The collision of thought and name thus produced for Jackie some remarkable successes. On one occasion Jeannie was a victim.

'The occasion,' said Jeannie in her book *Meet Me at the Savoy*, 'was the lunch given by the Foreign Press Association for the Archbishop of Canterbury. There was the usual busy round of table plans, lists of guests and paragraphs for the social columns. There was endless discussion as to the correct wording – did one put "Dr Temple, the Archbishop of Canterbury", "the Archbishop of Canterbury (Dr Temple)", or merely "the Archbishop of Canterbury"? In the end, I asked for a telephone call to be put through to the Dean. My head was still full of Archbishops and Primates when an awed secretary put her head round the door to say, "The Archbishop of Canterbury wishes to speak to you." That this was beyond the wildest bounds of probability did not occur to me and I picked up the receiver and began a long deferential monologue, which was answered by hoots of delighted laughter.

'Then I realised too late that I had given Jackie Broadbent one of his greatest triumphs!'

He was, despite his many friends, a lonely man. His marriage had gone astray many years before I first knew him; and his life had become a perpetual search for a permanent home. Yet, because of the wandering character of his profession he lived in hotels and furnished flats; and so he would soothe himself for having to put up with these temporary surroundings by assuring those who were listening: 'You wait for this time next year. I'll have a house of my own by then, and all my furniture and books will be out of store.' Unfortunately each year would materialise and find Jackie going on living in the same transient way. So it was this year.

He had been pensioned off, but he still had no permanent home.

'Well,' I said, picking up the telegram again after Jeannie had returned, 'what do we do?'

'It's a question of where we could put him.'

'He could sleep on a camp bed in the flower house.'

'He likes his comforts.'

'The main thing is how your mother would react.'

'She's always been fond of him.'

When we lived at Mortlake and had an annual party for the Boat Race, Monty sporting the pale blue of Cambridge around his neck as he sat in the window glaring at the crowds on the towpath, food for our guests used to be served at odd times because of the tide. Jeannie's mother and my own mother always used to be there but sometimes, although they said nothing to me or Jeannie, they used to become impatient. We would be engulfed by sophisticated friends, temporarily forgetting the two of them, when Jackie would suddenly appear at our side. And what he said at the first party became a routine joke for all the others. 'I think you ought to know,' he said solemnly, 'the Mums are hungry.'

I had a hunch we should invite him whatever the domestic difficulties. These, I believed, would solve themselves when helped by the gusto of the occasion; but this, of course, was a man's view. Jeannie, after all, was going to do all the work.

'Just think,' she said, 'of the number of people in the same mood as ourselves.'

'How do you mean?'

'All fussing on as to whether to ask this person or that for Christmas.'

'Darling Jeannie,' I said, retrieving the original subject, 'we have only one question to answer. What do we say in reply to Jackie's telegram?'

'Say yes.'

'You're sure?'

'Of course. I've the same hunch as you have.'

'I wonder why. He'd be self sufficient without us.'

'Isn't that the answer? Because he *would* be self sufficient, we're touched that he wants to come all the way to Minack. And perhaps we're apprehensive because of this.'

I reflect, sometimes, that omission rather than action has provided me with my chief regrets. There is a wilderness about omission. An instant flicks past your eyes demanding acknowledgement, and yet the mind fails to recognise it. There it is, an opportunity with all the shine on it yearning to beckon you, all your desires contained therein, all your striving on the edge of being rewarded, and yet your senses at this very moment of challenge betray you and make you fumble; and leave you with the hunger of what might have been.

When Jeannie's mother arrived we broke her the news.

'Jackie Broadbent is coming. I hope you don't mind.'

'It'll do him good.'

The reply was unexpected, and practical, and refreshing. And if it were short, this was compensated in a few moments when she added: 'What a true friend he has been to you both!'

'We'd have sent a wire stopping him if you'd said you wanted to be on your own.'

'Nonsense.'

There seemed now to be no irking doubt about this Christmas. It would have been easy for Jeannie's mother to have been distant in agreement, providing a cool edginess to pervade the holiday, the kind of remote disapproval that tediously destroys the pleasure of those present. For the power of the kill-joy is sinister in its effectiveness. He corrodes others who left on their own would be perfectly content. He can spoil a party or bring a rasping note into a holiday. And so he deserves harsh treatment if you have the courage to provide it. I know of a hotel proprietor who clinically watches the behaviour of his guests for the first three days of their stay; and if a detractor appears among them, he is politely asked to leave. 'You do not appear to be getting your money's worth,' he is suavely told, 'do please go somewhere else.' Most of us, however, would do nothing. We would prefer to suffer in silence rather than highlight a situation which was already distressing.

Lama, I soon realised, had ideas about being a kill-joy. She had watched the preparations suspiciously. She had been lifted off the bed in the spare room to make place for the aired sheets and blankets; and been dumped on the floor half asleep. She had observed the Christmas tree carried into the sitting room, and had been intrigued by the elaborate fuss that Jeannie had made of it; and she did not understand why, when she put out a paw to play with a bauble on a lower branch, she was firmly told to stop. Why this sudden discipline? And why all this brisk efficiency when normally it was a slow moving haphazard routine? She went into the flower house and looked for the pile of white packing paper on which it was so cosy to curl and doze, and found it gone. There was a surprising neatness about the shelves; and how was it that the gap in the corner beneath the desk which had been such a lucrative source of mice, had been blocked up? She had jumped on the camp bed, it was the same camp bed that Jeannie's father had used in the first World War, and jumped off again quickly. Obviously it was not up to her standard of comfort; but why was it there?

I do not know why it was that this Christmas Lama had hoped to be alone. But there is little doubt that she did. Perhaps it was that it had at last penetrated into her secret animal depths that she had found a home; and now, on longer an outsider, she was jealous of anything or anyone that appeared to threaten her security. She was certainly on guard. And when I remember the wild dangerous time of her kittenhood, I suppose there was reason for her to fear that the comfortable pace of her life was about to be taken away from her.

Anyhow she was about to take on the role of the kill-joy. And there was no ruthless person at Minack who would ask *her* to leave.

We, too, preferred to suffer in silence.

L-6

5

THE EAST wind blew on Christmas day, scything across the sea from the Lizard hidden in gloom. The black easterly. It slashed into our cliff, burning the meadows with the salt which came into it, tearing up the valley to the cottage, cutting into the cracks of window frames, rushing through the wood, screeching a message that bitter cold weather was upon us. And when Lama asked to be let out, and I opened the door and she gaily stepped outside, she suddenly stopped when her whiskers met the wind. Good gracious, no, she seemed to say to herself, *much* too cold; and immediately reversed into the cottage.

I heard Jeannie's mother call to me from the spare room: 'Merry Christmas!'

'Merry Christmas!' I replied, 'did you have a good sleep?'

Jeannie was with her and I listened to the murmur of their voices, and guessed they had already interchanged gifts. They were always in such a hurry it seemed to me, and I used to tease them by saying they were greedy. I liked to linger over present opening. I used to madden Jeannie by partly unwrapping a present, then getting up and filling and lighting a pipe and walking about the room before settling down again to the business of discovering what surprise awaited me. I wanted to prolong a pleasure which had taken so long to prepare.

Angus scampered in from the spare room, rushing up to me, then stopping at my feet, pushing his muzzle into my shoes, brown eyes glancing up at me, a gentle, hesitant whoof asking me to play. I pretended a savage kick at him, and he ran away, turned full circle, spread wide his front paws, and made again his token whoof. He had been to an elegant dog parlour before he set off on his holiday, and his coat had been trimmed to perfection. He looked particularly handsome. His loquacious stumpy tail, his shiny black coat, the dashing style of his whiskers and beard, proclaimed him as aristocrat of his breed; and there he was turning full circle again, then pouncing at my shoes and whoofing, and demanding a game which meant a chase up and down the room, a hide and seek between tables and chairs, an uproarious dog game of subtle give and take . . . when suddenly I became aware of a presence. Lama, with all the silent majesty of a sphinx, tip of tail flicking, was gazing at us. Not inquisitively. You had only to see her eyes. She was enraged.

I broke off from my toying with Angus; and courted her. She was sitting, with restrained fury, on the sofa. There was no comfort in fooling myself by thinking she was indulging in a feline pretence. Her back was straight, like Queen Victoria, and she was burning into the room the message: this is such an intolerable insult to my dignity that I can never forgive it. No right to play with Angus in front of me. How dare you!

I forthwith pushed Angus back into the spare room. No touchiness on his part. The game was over. He solidly, obediently returned to his rug. No complications at all. But Lama . . . I tried to lure her into being amused by poking a finger at her. I would gladly have accepted a nip from sharp teeth or a bash from a paw . . . but nothing. Here was a clear example of wounded vanity. No sycophancy from her. She was going to teach me a lesson that I must not take her good nature for granted.

She fell, of course, to my blandishments in the end. Or rather to Jeannie's. 'Come on Lama,' she called cheerfully, after I had explained what had happened, 'something special for you this morning.' And she held a saucer an inch above her little black nose. Aromas! Glorious greed! Let us forget what has happened! There, on the saucer, were the turkey giblets.

It was now my job to take Jackie Broadbent his morning tea. He had arrived in the late afternoon of Christmas Eve; and with him he had brought a leather valise like a cricket bag in which were his clothes for the stay, several half bottles of champagne and, carefully wrapped in greaseproof paper, a plucked pheasant.

There is a hazard about having a stove in the sitting room. Jeannie is watched. We have had guests who, instead of responding to my efforts to divert them, have preferred well meaningly to give Jeannie advice; a tendency, due perhaps to her gentleness, to influence her to cook *their* way, not hers. There are those who interfere with sauces. I have seen Jeannie happily stirring a long prepared sauce, then heard someone suggest she should add this or that to it; for it seems the sight of her at work, ever dodging our outstretched legs as we sip our drinks, impels good natured interference. She is so natural, so easy as she goes about her business, that people feel relaxed enough to comment. Some have claimed to be experts in the preparation of vegetables; and when Jeannie has been preparing peas, runner beans or potatoes in some perfectly straightforward manner, they have recounted with fervour the dish enjoyed in some delightful bistro. Salad snobs are, of course, the worst offenders. The sight of a lettuce makes them leap up, cry limited phrases of French, Spanish or Italian, demand out of the ordinary condiments, make huge play of the obvious task of rubbing garlic round a salad bowl; and, in fact, do all they can, innocently no doubt, to put Jeannie's good nature to flight. It is true, however, that Jeannie usually remains firm. It is also true, of course, that she is usually left in peace. But, in any case, it is always astonishing to me how she so serenely,

84

so without fuss, can conduct her preparations so calmly in front of the frivolous rest of us.

Jackie Broadbent's pheasant provided such frivolity. It was a meagre bird, already high, and certainly ready to be eaten; so Jeannie decided to cook it straight away for dinner.

'Cook it fast in a very hot oven,' demanded Jackie.

'Cook it slowly,' said Jeannie.

'Stuff it with mushrooms and butter,' urged Jackie.

'A pheasant shouldn't be stuffed,' answered Jeannie.

'Don't forget wafer thin potatoes, ma'am.'

'I agree.'

'Agree ma'am? Agree? Where's the champagne?'

He fancied himself as a cook and as a gourmet. He was one of those cooks who take elaborate care to preserve the stock from his cooking, the expert's base for another dish, and then finds he has kept it so long that it is bad when he needs it.

A cork popped.

'Anyhow,' I said, watching the glasses being filled and at the same time thinking of tomorrow's turkey, 'this pheasant is a useful trial run over the target.' Nobody heard me. Toasts were being drunk. All the wild laughter of easy companionship filled the cottage.

But this was one occasion when Jeannie surrendered the task of cooking. Jackie in due course said the pheasant was ready. Jeannie said it wasn't. And then from the spare room came the voice of her mother who was resting. 'Who is to be responsible for the pheasant when it's served?' I heard her call.

'Jackie!' answered Jeannie.

There was a chuckle and then the soft Scottish accent: 'Oh dear;' and she laughed again, comfortably and without malice, leaning her goodwill towards understanding Jackie's idiosyncrasies.

It was the worst cooked pheasant I have ever had.

But it had served its purpose. Jeannie now knew she had to be on her own when she cooked the Christmas dinner.

I took Jackie his morning tea, and because there was frost in the wind, Jeannie had filled a thermos. I carried it with a cup down the path and across to the flower house wondering whether, in this cold, Jackie had slept a wink. I opened the door and wished him Merry Christmas, but there was no reply. The camp bed stretched low along the floor and above it were the shelves, usually filled with jam jars and galvanised pails holding the wallflowers and marigolds and forget-me-nots, but now bare. The bedclothes were pulled up to his eyes and I thought he was asleep, and without trying to wake him I bent down and lit the two paraffin stoves which stood by the door. I felt the heat suddenly emerging from them, and knowing the room would soon be warm and that the tea would remain hot in the thermos, I decided to leave him. I opened the door.

'Come back!'

'Good heavens, Jackie, I thought you were asleep.'

I picked up the thermos, unscrewed the top and poured out the tea. 'Merry Christmas!' I said. Then I added, laughing, 'So you were wide awake all the time I was looking after your welfare lighting the stoves.'

'Wide awake? I've been wide awake all night. What else do you expect a man to do lying on a bed belonging to World War One, reminding him of the idiocy of the human race?'

'Sorry it was so uncomfortable.'

'Forty-five years ago men slept on this bed dreaming of the greatness of the British Empire, girls, drink, white supremacy, the glory of dying for a brave new world, contentment, riches, all the delusions that lead men to their end.'

'You *are* cheerful.'

'I'm so cheerful I could dance.' And he kicked his legs up and down under the bed clothes. I feared the camp bed might collapse.

'Anyhow it's Christmas.'

'Don't be so sentimental. Three quarters of the world have never heard of Christmas.'

I had seen him in this mood many times before. I used to see him in the flat he had in Buckingham Gate, sitting propped up in bed pouring out these diatribes, superficially so bitter, but, if the truth be told, in justification of his own idealism; a consequence, I suppose, of prolonged observation as to how history is made.

'Give me my pipe and tobacco pouch. There . . . on the shelf behind you.'

He had levered himself up from the bedclothes. There was a scarf round his neck, and he wore his overcoat.

'Oh dear,' said the host in me, 'you must have been terribly cold. I'll light the stove for you tonight.'

'And asphyxiate me with their fumes. No thanks . . . ' the.. he added gently, 'I'm all right, don't bother.'

He lit his pipe, puffed it until the smoke billowed, then took it out of his mouth, and stabbed it towards me.

'What about the tea?' I interrupted, 'it'll be tepid.'

'Never mind the tea,' he answered abruptly, 'I'm in the mood to give you a lecture.'

'Oh lord.'

'Listen,' he said, 'as I lay shivering in this bed I heard the guns of Passchendaele. The primitive guns which could only kill a dozen at a time, perhaps two, perhaps more, it doesn't matter. And I saw the leaders of opinion, the usual lot . . . the politicians hiding behind generals, the churchmen, the societies which are manipulated by local ambitious men and women. I saw them not only in this country but in all countries. There they were, all desperately earnest in their fashion, intoxicated by a flag and a symbol, simple people elevated by luck to leadership of the rabble. All of them both sides, were sincere in committing their faults or virtues. But . . . ' and he now realised his pipe had gone out and stopped talking to light it again, ' . . . but . . . that generation which slept on beds like this one were only *toying* with war.'

'Obviously,' I said calmly, 'despite the losses.'

'Yes, yes, I know the point you're making . . . but don't you see that the minds of men and women haven't kept pace with the machines of war?'

'I do,' I said, 'but minds never have done.'

'Ah,' he said, 'you're thinking I'm talking about the Great Powers. I am not. They have their own histories to guide them and steer them clear of trouble unless there is an accident. Mark my words . . . Russia will come to terms with America before long. They're safe. It's the juvenile governments I'm thinking of. No history to guide them, no Passchendaele to tell *them* of war. An atom bomb is a plaything in their primitive political struggles, a trivial ally to their shouts. Sooner or later the Bomb will be the revolutionary weapon. It will *not* be the deterrent. That's what I was thinking about on this Passchendaele bed.'

'On Christmas day.'

'Shut up.'

One of the endearing characteristics of Jackie Broadbent was that, after working himself up into an emotion which might daunt a listener, he would suddenly change his tack. It would be done with such flair and gaiety that laughter would immediately follow tension This was such an occasion. He was suddenly no longer interested in the symbolic chance of sleeping on a World War One camp bed.

'I'm going to surprise Jeannie's mother,' he said like a conspirator, 'by taking her a half bottle of Moet et Chandon for her breakfast.'

'You won't surprise her.'

'Why?' And he sounded disappointed.

'I think she would only be surprised if you didn't.'

6

AT MID-DAY my cousin Carol arrived from his home near St Just, holding a red and green knitted tea cosy in his arms. He took great enjoyment from making small incidents into dramas and I sensed that this was one of them. He was highly excited.

'Merry Christmas! Merry Christmas!' Then, the formality over, he hastily added: 'I have a surprise for you. Where's Jeannie?'

'But you've given us your presents.'

'Ah,' he said, still standing in the doorway, 'I've got something else.'

'Jeannie!' I called, 'Carol's here with a mystery!' Then turning to him: 'We're having the turkey for dinner. Only cold meat for lunch.'

I realised, before disclosing the purpose of the tea cosy, he wanted a full audience; and so he also required the presence of Jeannie's mother and Jackie. Fortunately the three of them appeared from the spare room together.

I watched the delight on Carol's face. Here was the big moment, Harlequin's triumph. The audience titillated into expectation, the mystery still in his keeping; all that was now required was the exact timing of its disclosure.

'Carol,' I said gently, 'there is a bitter east wind, you're still standing at the door . . . and the sitting room will soon be a refrigerator.'

'All right, all right,' he said jokingly, though lowered a

little by my remarks, 'let me take my time . . . my time!'

He now advanced into the cottage, the tea cosy cradled in his arms; then, as I quickly shut the door, he paused for a second in the middle of the room, looked round at our faces, and declared with the dramatic effect of a magician:

'I hold in this tea cosy . . . a blackbird!'

He achieved, without doubt, his triumph. We imagined I think, that it was to be a gimmick joke, some idiotic foolery which, unless one was in the mood of carnival, deserved only forced laughter. This was indeed unexpected, and there was immediate consternation from Jeannie.

'Here, look at it,' said Carol.

Apparently he had been sitting in the ground floor room of his Nanquidno house when there was a bang on the window. He looked up and was in time to see a bird fall to the ground. He rushed out and found a blackbird stunned into lifelessness.

'The only idea I had,' he explained, 'was that I must keep it warm. So I tucked it into this tea cosy, got Tara into the car, and rushed over.'

Jeanne had dealt with many stunned birds before. They sometimes, alas, fly into the clear glass of our greenhouses, especially in the spring when the young are learning to fly. And she has formed a procedure which is infallible in bringing them back to consciousness, and healing them provided no organic damage has been done. She always keeps ready a concoction called Exultation of Flowers, a medicine which comes from the Scottish Highlands, a secret mixture containing the juices from a wide variety of flowers. She opens the beak of the bird, puts a drop or two down its throat, and within a few seconds it begins to revive.

And so this was how she treated Carol's blackbird. But the effect on it was so remarkable that within a minute or so it started to struggle, then a moment later escaped from her hand, flew round the room and landed on top of the Christmas tree. It was another five minutes before she managed to catch it again, and she did so when it perched on the mistletoe in the porch. It was easy then, and she opened the door and let it fly out; and for a long time afterwards a blackbird with a splendid yellow beak haunted the bird table. Clougy, we called it, after the name of Carol's home.

Lama, at the time, was curled on our bed, and she chose to wake up, stretch herself, and come into the sitting room at the moment Carol was entering with Tara. The old lady looked at her as if she were saying: 'Don't worry, little cat. I'm much too old to cause you any worry.' Such condescending good nature would have been effective had Lama been frightened. She was not. It was obvious to us that her only emotion was suspicion. First Angus, now this huge Alsatian: what's up? She also observed that Jeannie and I had made an extravagant fuss of the dog; and out of the corner of my eye I caught a dirty look from her, and felt sure she was thinking: 'Traitor!'

But Tara was indeed remarkable. She was now nearly fourteen years old, and so good tempered, so beautiful to look at, that it would be impossible not to admire her; and part of this admiration was due to her owner who never inflicted her on others. She might be very old. She might need special attention. But in one of those uncanny relationships between man and beast, they understood they must share the pain with each other. The outsiders could never understand. Thus, much better to be silent and not try to persuade them. For Tara had often been to Minack; but had remained, at Carol's insistence, in his car. Never before had she faced Lama inside her own home.

It was now that Angus scampered in from the spare room, took one look at Tara, and scampered back again. Meanwhile Lama had moved to beneath my desk and was crouched there, scowling. I felt certain we were in for trouble. There was Tara spreading herself in the centre of

91

the room, Angus becoming excited; and the owner of the premises loathing them both.

'Don't you think,' I asked nervously, 'that we ought to keep them separated?'

Nobody heard me. Nobody wanted to hear me. Jeannie and her mother were perfectly confident. I was only a fusspot. And as for the other two, they were at the sideboard. Jackie was opening the champagne.

There was no trouble. There was only a certain unease. Tara and Angus tolerated each other, Lama did not attack either of them. But Lama, I well knew, was thoroughly irritated. No room on the sofa, too much noise, Angus nosing at her plate, Tara enveloping the space, *her* space, in front of the electric fire, and a casual attitude from Jeannie and me. We didn't mean to be casual, we were just enjoying ourselves.

And Lama displayed her irritation throughout the afternoon in a most effective way.

'Lama what *are* you up to?'

I knew, of course, very well. She was at the window asking to be let out, three minutes after being let in, because she was at a loss to know what to do with herself. Outside much too cold, inside the role of the unwilling hostess.

One moment hypnotising me with amber eyes through the glass, the next impelling me by a vigorous swishing of her tail to let her out again. It was a shrewd way of emphasising her displeasure that routine had been disrupted.

Dusk fell early that Christmas day, darkened by the weather across the bay towards the Lizard. There was the bitter wind; and the huge bank of fog and gloom hiding the distant land; and in contrast the grey heaving sea seemed to have surprisingly white horses, gay to look at, dashing at each other, bursting into spray, re-grouping together and advancing in a long line, this ribbon of white which dissolved so soon into the grey, rough mass which was its home. Snow was coming, I felt sure, and if it didn't arrive tonight it would be with us in the morning. There was a menacing cruelty outside the cottage; and I knew that if we had been alone, without diversions, Jeannie and I would have been pacing the meadows, vacantly, uselessly, anticipating disaster, assessing in our minds that there would be no flowers for the posies, if snow came.

It was time to shut up Boris, and this time I opened the door and went out with Lama, then down the path across the grass by the greenhouse and into the wood. There in the old chicken house, the size of a palace as far as Boris is concerned, room for thirty muscovy drakes not one, sat Boris on his perch craning his neck forwards and gently hissing. 'Good night, Boris,' I said, and locked the door. He was such an imperious character that one felt in duty bound to say the words, 'good night'; and sometimes when I had absent-mindedly forgotten to do so, I used foolishly to return and shout the words through the door. As if it were a talisman of good luck to wish him good night.

I had turned and was on my way back to the cottage when, by the entrance of the flower house, I saw a shadow at my feet and there was Lama. Shelagh had given us a photograph of Lama as a Christmas present, a photograph she had secretly taken of her sitting on the white seat by the verbena bush during the summer; and then had framed. Jane's present had been a set of small glasses on each of which she had painted a cat in silver paint. And she had given me a spell. Once, after a long hot day digging potatoes down the cliff, I held up a glass of water and said to Jane, her long fair hair falling over her shoulders: 'Be a witch, Jane. Cast a spell. Turn this glass of water into a bottle of wine!' I often asked her to cast a spell at the work's end.

I picked up Lama and began to carry her up to the door. I had not gone far before she began to struggle, and to squeak, like the noise of a high note on an out-of-tune violin. 'Lama,'

I said, 'you *are* unsociable.' And I put her on the ground, and saw her dash back down the path, then disappear round the corner. She's gone into the old stables, I said to myself, out of the wind.

Inside the cottage was the quiet time of Christmas. Too much at lunch had been caught up by tea; and there was the pause, the interval in which the hilarious gaiety of lunch-time impatiently awaits the start of the preliminaries before dinner. Jackie was at my desk reading a book like a school-boy, hands over ears. Jeannie's mother sat on the sofa, Angus as her feet, knitting a jersey for Jeannie's sister, talking to my cousin Carol beside her, and eyeing Jeannie at the pantry. Jeannie was preparing the turkey.

She followed a Scottish recipe. She stuffed the turkey, made a dough of flour and water, rolled it out an inch thick, covered the turkey with fat bacon and butter, then wrapped the dough round it like a blanket; not a centimetre of the turkey visible. Then the turkey went into the oven for three hours, after which the dough casing was easily lifted off, and the turkey basted and left to brown for half an hour. This was her proven way of doing it.

'Keep Jackie out of the way,' she murmured to me.

'I overheard that, ma'am.'

'Thought you were reading, Jackie.'

'No, ma'am.'

'It was that pheasant, Jackie. We don't want the turkey like the pheasant.'

'No ma'am.'

When Jackie was contrite, one wasn't sure whether he was laughing or not.

'We'll go down to the pub,' I said, 'then we'll all be out of your way, Jeannie.'

'And Carol,' she said, 'can have the job of seeing you're back by eight.'

'No ma'am.'

'Silly fool, Jackie.'

'Yes, ma'am.'

We were back punctually at eight. We came back and found the cottage lit by candlelight, the Christmas tree in its corner sparkling its baubles, shadows touching the white, rough walls making them appear like crumpled cloth, a single candle in the old baking oven lighting the dome of patchwork stones, the outline of holly in odd places, and staring down at us softly from the wall on the way to the spare room was Jeannie's wistful, gentle portrait by Kanelba.

Here was the setting, the everlasting setting of Christmas; unabashed affection for each other, age no hindrance, the intellect momentarily defeated and emotion for the time being supreme, hard men kind, the mean pushed to display generosity, jealousy in abeyance, greed despicable, heightened awareness towards those you love, tenderness towards those taken for granted. This was the ancient shine which suffused the cottage as we laughed and rejoiced and shouted our way through Christmas dinner.

'To Jeannie's mother!'

'To Jeannie!'

'To Carol!'

'To Jackie!'

It was at that moment that my own toast was about to be proposed . . . that I remembered Lama. I had not seen her since I put Boris to bed. I had ignored her existence. First the pub, then our wonderful dinner; and we had all forgotten her. Dogs had been cared for. The hostess ignored.

'Where are you going?'

I had suddenly, without explanation, rushed to the door.

'Wait!' I said, 'until I come back!'

'Why?' asked Jeannie.

'I have to find Lama.'

I paused and looked at Jeannie. She was laughing.

'Why laugh?' I asked doubtfully, a sixth sense warning me that I was making a fool of myself.

'Idiot!' she said, 'I brought her in long ago. She's on the bed deep in a turkey sleep!'

I quickly recovered my composure and went back to my seat. Of course I should have known about Jeannie. Busy as she was, gay as the rest of us, she would have remembered.

I picked up my glass and raised it towards her, smiling.

'To Lama!' I said.

'To Lama!' called everyone else.

At this moment, like an actress making an entrance, she appeared from the bedroom, plump, a sleepy, benign little black cat. She gazed round for a second, then tucking her head into her chest, she collapsed and rolled on her back on the carpet.

She was content.

She, too, had been captured by the Christmas spirit.

FOUR YEARS LATER

1

ONE LOVELY October morning Lama had come for a stroll with me, treating it as usual as an affair of fits and starts; one moment trotting quietly at my heels, another moment dashing like a mad cat ahead of me, the next dallying so far behind that she chose to hold me by letting loose a series of heartrending miaows. She had been at Minack for over six years and there was now no evidence that she had ever been a wild cat. Rough edges had been smoothed. Subtle tricks of domestic cats had been acquired. And quite clearly she seemed to think that she was in a cat-like heaven where no one ever meant any harm to each other. No longer was she on guard for danger in every second. She was serene. She loved everyone and everything. Indeed, her supreme confidence, her belief that you only have to offer goodwill, for goodwill to be offered in return, often caused us anxiety. I saw her once lying in the lane beside the stream, while on the other side of the stream sat a fox cub. Lama looked round and saw it, then nonchalantly got up and walked towards it. The cub fled.

Our principal concern was her attitude to the donkeys. We had acquired Penny, the mother, by chance. She was black with grey underbelly, and with a very handsome head; but when we first saw her in a field adjacent to a pub near Redruth, she looked moth eaten, bare patches on her coat, elongated hooves like Dutch clogs and an appeal in her eyes which Jeannie interpreted as: 'Buy me please.' The publican, who was a dealer in horses and donkeys, and who had only quartered Penny for a few days or so, then gave us a further piece of information. Penny was in foal, and the foal was expected within a month. 'Two donkeys for one!' had laughed Roy Teague, the publican. I had gone out for a quiet drink; but when I returned to Minack, Penny was in the back of the Land Rover.

The foal was born according to schedule. He arrived in a deluge of rain on a flat stone in the big field; and he was, of course, enchanting. He was perky and vulnerable, toy-like and laughable; he had a pretty head with huge ears like old fashioned motoring gloves, fluffy brown coat, a short box of a body on spindly legs, and a look in his eyes that made me smile when I first saw it. He looked so gay. He was so ridiculously happy; and then suddenly, perhaps due to his surprise at seeing us, he lost his balance and col-lapsed on the ground. Tiny hooves tried to get a grip on the grass, then he gave a lurch, and he was upright again. A slight loss of confidence, a sense of indignity, of having made a fool of himself; and then once again he looked mis-chievous. We called him Fred.

Fred was now three years old. For the first two years of his life he was like a prince with an endless number of courtiers. Children came hurrying down the lane with lumps of sugar and carrots, a party was held for him on his first birthday, cameras were constantly poised pointing at him, extravagant praises were showered upon him, faces of grown ups melted at the sight of him, adulation, the glory of a child film star, innocence, flattery, hardly a day passing without some admirer paying court to him. He revelled in it; and he responded by gently allowing small arms to be flung around his neck and showing no impatience when his ears were stroked and his soft nose hugged. As far as he was concerned this attention would go on for ever; but there came the awful moment of truth. A visitor looked at the now gawky teenager of a donkey and said: 'I prefer the other one!'

Penny had come into her own again.

Penny was certainly a beautiful donkey with a coat which was now shiny black, and a head which, when alerted, reminded one of an Arab pony. She was placid; and when the children came to see Fred, it was Penny who gave them their rides. We would lead her up and down the field, sometimes one sometimes two on her back, while Fred frisked beside her. She was like a beach donkey, resigned to her duties to give pleasure; and indeed an attitude of resignation was a feature of Penny for a long while after her arrival at Minack. It was as if she could not make herself believe it to be true that she had at last found a permanent home. She had been for so long an itinerant donkey, first in Ireland then in this country, receiving affection only so long as it suited her owner, that she seemed to be daily waiting for her next move. Then it gradually dawned on her that she was here to stay, and that Fred was to stay too; and she began to acquire some of Fred's gaiety.

Lama's behaviour towards them was foolhardy.

'Look at Lama!' I had shouted in fright a day or two after Penny's arrival at Minack. Penny, in the middle of a meadow, was peacefully munching the grass. Lama was there too. She was gently rubbing herself against a hind leg, treating it as if it were a post.

Penny's detachment on this occasion, her apparent acceptance of a cat behaving in such a familiar fashion, led Lama to believe that she would always be welcome. Here was an opportunity for Lama to display the trust she possessed in such abundance. Why should she worry about a donkey's kick? Or being stepped on by a heavy hoof? This confidence was no doubt justified as far as Penny was concerned. Penny took Lama for granted; to Penny, Lama was just a little black cat which sometimes happened to be in the way. She had no special interest in her.

Fred, on the other hand, was fascinated. It is a fascination which has never dimmed since first we introduced Lama to him when he was one day old. On that occasion we lifted Lama up to his face, and she licked his nose; and when we put her to the ground again, Fred tried to do the same to her. Such affection, however, had to be balanced by realism; for though Lama remained the same size, Fred of course grew and grew until he became like a rock compared to a pebble. Lama and Fred might not see the danger in the situation. We did. And therefore Jeannie and I became sometimes distraught by the cajoling antics they displayed towards each other.

Lama had no imagination. If, for instance, Fred was in one meadow and I was taking him to another, I would find Lama sitting directly on our path.

'Out of the way, Lama,' I would call, 'shoo!'

Not the slightest notice.

At the sight of her Fred would have put his head down, and be straining at the halter. Then, as we closed within a few feet, his pace would quicken and I would try to hold him.

'Get out of the way, Lama!' I would shout. And then, as if all the time she had been teasing, Lama *would* dash from the giant which was Fred.

There was no harm in Fred. True I have known him behave coltishly, but this was always due to someone treating him too casually; treating him, in fact, as Lama treated him. Fred simply did not know his own strength; and so we feared for Lama when she behaved towards him as if he were a playmate of her own size. We also laughed. It was an absurd sight watching Fred catch sight of Lama on the other side of a field, then go cantering towards her, a frolic of a canter, full of joyous anticipation of a game, while Lama waited for him playing her own version of Russian roulette. Fred was always so ludicrously anxious to reach her. Lama in a field, Lama on a wall within possible touch of him,

Lama on the path in front of him . . . Fred never failed to express an extrovert's delight in seeing her; while Lama, trusting Lama, never in the end trusted Fred quite enough. She was away within a split second of his arrival.

On that October morning when Lama and I were going for a stroll, the donkeys were in a field above the cottage. Fred had now outgrown his gawkiness, and shed his shaggy brown youthful coat, and looked a little thoroughbred; and he was receiving again the attention he so enjoyed. He had grown larger than Penny, and his coat was a cocoa colour, and time and again admirers would say: 'Look at his cross!' It was a beautiful black cross, one line tracing the length of his backbone and dissolving into his tail; the other two branching from it at the nape of his neck, each fingering down his shoulders. 'Why is it there?' the few who did not know its tradition would ask. 'Donkeys are blessed,' I would reply, 'because Jesus chose a donkey on which to ride into Jerusalem.'

I left the donkeys staring down from their field into the small garden outside the door of the cottage, standing side by side, ears erect, inquisitive. 'The donkeys are wanting something,' I called to Jeannie. 'All right,' she replied, 'I'll give them a chocolate biscuit in a moment.' I walked away down the path then right through the white gate to the big field; and then right again along the track towards the small field facing the sea which has been known since time immemorial as the onion meadow. On either side of the track, in early spring, bloomed bed upon bed of daffodils. There was the meadow of a beautiful daffodil with the ugly classified name of Sulphur, so ugly that when as an experiment we changed the name to Lamorna, the price jumped by a shilling a bunch. Further on there was a meadow of California and opposite, on the other side of the track, a meadow of the large yellow trumpet called Rembrandt; and beside it, another containing the fragrant white Actaea with its red

104

centre. As it was autumn, feet high grass still covered the meadows, but soon it would be cut and the ground rotavated; and by Christmas we would be watching the green heralds of the flowers poking up from the soil.

I paused every few yards waiting for Lama to catch up with me, and when I reached the onion meadow I sat down on a low stone hedge; and a minute later she had jumped up on my knees, settling herself like a glossy black cushion, and began gently to purr. It was a heavenly day, a day when the sea was a cornflower blue; and fringing the arm of the Lizard across the Bay was a billowy line of white clouds. The sun shone on the long stretch of sands at Looe Bar, and below me a few hundred yards off shore there were a half dozen small boats grouped together, with tiny figures leaning over their sides feathering a shoal of mackerel. It was very still, an Indian summer day; and to my left was Carn Barges, a huge rock balanced upright as if it were a sentinel. Beyond was Carn Dhu which juts out from the far side of Lamorna Cove, sheltering the Cove with high, grey boulder strewn cliffs, this lovely cove which on a day like this has the stillness of a South Sea lagoon; and for ever reminds me of Cook's Bay in Moorea. I sat there listening to the curlews calling as they swept across the sky high above me, to a robin singing a sad song, to the sudden laugh of a green woodpecker which see-sawed its way inland to my right, to the throb of a French crabber with emerald green hull heading for Newlyn, to the sea touching the rocks like the swish of a gentle wind through trees; and to Lama purring.

This was one of those naïve moments when one would like to tear away from their anchors the sad and the tired and the bored; to refresh and awaken them by the feel of a Cornish day when the sea is a cornflower blue. Here is a gift which has no need of man's interference. Here is permanence, the unending bridge between the past and the present which gives the human soul its base. Brains are no asset at such a moment. All that is required is an attitude of mind which is capable of exultation, a heart that soars as it watches, a human being who has purged himself of aiming to conquer by logic. No brittle questions need be asked. No detached observance. Just the ability to catch the fleeting awareness that there can be moods which do not belong to reason. Another dimension enters your life amid the solitude and the grandeur; and suddenly there is a stranger within yourself.

I had sat there perhaps five minutes when Lama suddenly became alert, flapping her tail urgently against my arm; and the purring stopped. Thirty yards below me on a rock I saw the cause. A small grey cat was crouched there watching us.

I had seen this cat from time to time over the years. It was obviously wild and I did not see it often; but from time to time one of us would catch it unawares on the cliff, and whoever had seen it, would say later to the other: 'I saw the little grey cat today.' Or when we did not see it for a long time, sooner or later we would say, 'I wonder what's happened to it?'

It never showed the slightest interest in us. Indeed it ran away into the undergrowth if ever we called to it, or even if it only saw us. But on this occasion, as it crouched on the rock, it continued quietly to watch me; and after a while Lama relaxed, the tail stopped flapping, a purr began again.

I wondered why.

2

MY AUNT, my eighty-two-year-old aunt, was late in coming to stay at Minack that year. She had taken a motor coach excursion trip to Baden Baden in the spring, had another excursion for ten days on the Italian lakes in the autumn, and in between had visited Coventry Cathedral, Osterley Park, the Runnymede RAF Memorial, a number of theatres, Kew Gardens more than once, several exhibitions, and had remained glued to her television set throughout the Wimbledon fortnight. She arrived at Minack, elegant, informed, and sparkling with enthusiasm for life. She was a lesson as to how to grow old; contemporary in thought, historically knowledgeable, self-sufficient yet a stimulating companion, she had only one flaw. Lama. She and Lama could never come to terms. Neither of them, however hard they tried, could entirely relax in each other's company.

'Pussoo,' coaxed my aunt in her usual way on arrival in the cottage, and in what she thought was an appealing tone, 'come here, pussoo, come here to me.' And she bent down and held out her hand. 'Dear pussoo. Be friendly, pussoo.'

I silently prayed that Lama would respond and behave like a charming hostess, but I also knew there was a snag. It was obvious that Lama did not approve of the word pussoo. She thought it childish, condescending and over-familiar. Why should this comparative stranger arrive for a stay, and forthwith burble such nonsense at her?

'Now don't be rude, pussoo. Come and say how do you do.'

Lama was sitting with her back to the stove, her tail wrapped round her so that the silky black tip gently flicked against a front paw. She stared loftily at my aunt. A cool, superior gaze, like a dowager putting a gauche guest in her place. 'I do not obey orders,' she seemed to be saying, 'I am a cat . . . not a dog.'

My aunt, with her affinity towards dogs, was at a loss as to what to do next. A dog came to her, wagging its tail, smiling, welcoming, at the snap of a finger and thumb, even a dog she had never met before. She liked such friendliness. It was effortless. So much more pleasant than the behaviour of a little black cat which defied her well meaning approaches.

'Selfish breed,' my aunt said crossly, thinking of all the cats she had casually known, 'you come from a very selfish breed, Lama.' Thereupon she left Lama to ponder over such a remonstrance, and retired to her room.

The fact was, however, that my aunt and Lama both had the same basic intentions. Each wanted to win the other on their own terms. My aunt, for instance, longed to see Lama responding to discipline like a dog; a misguided ambition, of course, but one that is common among those who have never understood cats. I once felt the same myself. It maddened me that I should be patronised, defied, ignored, by such an arrogant domestic animal; and thus, although no longer that way inclined, I *understood* my aunt.

Lama, meanwhile, had her own frustrations. She observed my aunt's methods of courting, and thought it surprising. For she had discovered, in her time, that human beings could be divided into two sections; either they were slaves to her whims, or they completely ignored her existence. Yet here was a third section. Here was someone who clearly wished to gain her approval, in fact was most anxious to do so; why go such an unusual way about it? Lama was prepared to be lured, but not to be ordered; and she also was ready to be flattered providing the flattery was subtly paid. Hence, had my aunt walked across the room to *her*, pleasing Lama by such a touch of courtesy, my aunt would have been rewarded by some gentle accolade such as a purr or a rub round her legs. Lama, however, did not realise that such accolades did not rank high in my aunt's estimation. My aunt, for instance, would have been horrified had Lama rubbed round her legs, while Lama would have been quite certain she was bestowing a great honour. Indeed, it was this gulf in values that was the cause of the trouble between them. Both were being thwarted. My aunt by being unable to impose her will on Lama, Lama by being unable to bewitch my aunt.

Both of them, however, were unperturbed by the initial setback. My aunt continued to operate her direct tactics, while Lama set out to *cajole* my aunt into submission. And the cajoling was performed in the most delightful way, delightful that is, to anyone who appreciated a cat's special attention.

Lama, for instance, would pay my aunt the compliment of jumping on her bed when my aunt was not in the room; and curling up in a tight black ball on my aunt's pink satin nightdress. My aunt, when she found out the situation, did not see the gesture as a compliment. In her view Lama, like all cats, was an unclean thing . . . and the sight of Lama on the bed, on her nightdress, greatly distressed her. Get off! Get off! And Lama would find herself unceremoniously dumped on the floor, not understanding what all the fuss was about, but vaguely aware that she had once again failed to bewitch my aunt.

There were other gestures on the part of Lama which my aunt misunderstood. On those days when Lama was left out in pouring rain, designedly on her part because she was on some mouse catching business, she would in due course re-enter the cottage by jumping on the window sill and staring at us, slit amber eyes in a black face, until she gained our attention. She would then have the pleasure of seeing one of us rush to open the door; and both of us giving her a wonderful welcome. Poor Lama, soaking wet, feel her fur! At this stage she would be immediately aware that we were competing, Jeannie and I, for her favours. She would be about to lick herself dry, a lap was the most suitable place for the exercise; and would it be mine or would it be Jeannie's?

Having observed this competition between us, Lama came to the conclusion that the act of drying herself, of depositing her wet person on a lap, was a gesture which gave considerable pleasure. Why not, then, ring the changes and give my aunt the chance of feeling rain sodden fur, or watching the busy lick at close quarters, of relaxing in the aftermath of a cat's outing in the rain?

So there was my aunt sitting comfortably on the sofa reading a newspaper, and there was Lama like a wet black sponge at her feet. I watched Lama glance up at the skirt which appeared beneath the newspaper. A moment's thought. Yes, I will give her the honour. Leap!

Newspaper, Lama, my aunt crashed together . . . and a second later Lama was on the floor again.

Her most foolish gesture towards my aunt, however, was yet to come. Heaven knows what prompted her to make it because it was exceedingly rare that she ever made it to Jeannie and me. Once during the summer it had happened and I had given her a rapturous welcome; but the circumstances had been somewhat exceptional. It was a hot June afternoon and I had chosen to take pen and paper down the cliff to a meadow which was perched close to the sea. I had been down there some time when, at the exact moment when I was trying to write about her, Lama appeared at my feet. She looked up at me enquiringly. In her mouth was a mouse.

The first part of this story was told to me later by Jeannie. She had been spending the afternoon pottering about the garden and had noticed that Lama was having an especially fruitful period of hunting. She said that she had seen her devour three mice to her certain knowledge, and then catch a fourth; and the last Jeannie saw of the fourth was when Lama busily set off down the path towards the big field and the cliff with the mouse still firmly in her mouth. How did she know where I was? And how does one explain the coincidence that she arrived when she did?

I was, needless to say, flattered by such a gesture. My aunt, when it happened to her, was not. She was sitting in the greenhouse protected from a cold autumn wind and catching the warmth of the fading sun, sitting at ease in a deck chair, when Lama appears through the doorway, prances up to her, and with a wild little cry deposits a capture, at her feet.

'Oh, dear, she's going to eat it,' said my aunt, gathering herself in the deck chair, a note of despair in her voice, 'drat you, Lama, I was so enjoying myself. You're a beastly, sadistic cat!'

And off went my aunt, leaving Lama, a puzzled playful Lama in possession of the greenhouse.

These collisions between the two of them, however, were not so disastrous as they might first appear. Lama, in good faith, made misjudgments in her effort to cajole my aunt which might have permanently offended any other cat-hater. I am quite sure, in my time as a cat-hater, I would have shown no patience at all. Lama would have conformed to my worst opinion of cats and in those days I would have found no excuse for her behaviour. I would have labelled her selfish and disruptive. I would have disapproved of those who fussed over her. I would have been glad to have left her environment.

My aunt was more objective in her attitude. Lama had

grace. Lama might have her faults, in my aunt's opinion, which belonged to all her breed; but she possessed an elusive quality, a subtle femininity, which fascinated my aunt. Thus despite disapproving of her actions, my aunt became fonder of Lama the more she saw of her. Prejudice against the breed did not mean prejudice against Lama. Indeed I found myself thinking that here was a lesson. My aunt, in these lightsome forays with Lama, proved that one should never confuse convictions with individuals. A cat-hater can always be charmed by a cat.

3

SOON AFTER my aunt had returned to London, I saw the grey cat again. Jeannie was with me this time. It was the second week of November.

'We must make up our minds about this year's Christmas card,' Jeannie had said at breakfast, 'or we'll be in a panic again.'

'What do you suggest?'

We aimed each year to have a photograph of some part of our life at Minack.

'Well,' said Jeannie, 'last year it was the coloured one of the daffodils in the stable meadow with the cottage in the background. The year before we left it too late and had to buy a ready made one. The year before that was me and the donkeys.'

I had always liked that one. It was the year Fred was born; and the Christmas card was a picture of Jeannie riding Penny while holding Fred, a very small Fred, by his halter.

'What about a photograph of Lama?' I said. Four years before, the Christmas card had been a picture of Jeannie and me with Lama in Jeannie's arms. It was not a very good photograph. Lama looked like a black spot against Jeannie's white jersey.

'Possibly,' said Jeannie doubtfully.

'What's the objection?'

'I just feel,' said Jeannie, picking up the egg cups and carrying them to the sink, 'that it ought to be the donkeys again. It's their year after all.'

It was true that scores of people had come to see them that summer.

'You may be right.'

'And I've an idea,' went on Jeannie, 'of the photograph you could take of them.'

'What's that?'

I have no pretensions about my photography. I point my camera at the object, suffer difficulty in focusing, then trust that the automatic lightmeter will operate correctly.

'I thought we might take the donkeys to Carn Barges,' explained Jeannie, 'and then you can photograph them silhouetted against the background of our bay.'

The bay was a teaspoon of a bay at the foot of our cliff meadows, a crevice of water where often we would find a seal, only face and moustache in sight, swaying with the waves, aware that he was safe as we stood on our rocks and gazed at him.

'It's a good idea,' I said, 'and we can go straight away. The sun rising up above the Lizard will be behind me, and it will be a lovely walk, and we can think of the world rushing to their offices while we have the freedom to set off on this ozone filled sunny morning with a couple of donkeys along a path above the sea.'

Carn Barges, the formation of rocks falling steeply down to the sea which we looked out upon across the moorland from the cottage, was jokingly called by us the near feeding grounds. Around the topmost rocks were succulent grasses which the donkeys much enjoyed. They would nibble away, etched against the skyline while the fishing boats passed by below them; and sometimes a man from a fishing-boat would cup his hands together and shout a greeting, and the donkeys would prick up their ears and stare back at him inquisitively.

Then there were also the far feeding grounds. These were further on, along a tortuous path towards Lamorna, and when the donkeys were in an adventurous mood the walk could be a hazardous affair. We walked in single file, Jeannie and I first, then the donkeys, free of their halters. Usually they followed in docile fashion, leisurely partaking of any greenery they fancied on the way; but there were occasions when they were boisterous, as if they were egging each other on to play a joke on us. And sometimes in this mood they caught us unawares, and barged past us, and in a second they would be racing along the path which led away from the moorland and on to the road which fell down the side of the valley to Lamorna village. Perhaps it was the pub they were aiming for. From time to time we would take them sedately by their halters; and while we sipped beer, they would eat potato crisps. But they have never been on their own yet. We have always caught them in time.

At the start of a walk, as they went past the garden and across the expanse of the big field, we always kept them under control by their halters; and only let them run free when they had clambered over the boundary hedge and were on the narrow path which was edged on either side by undergrowth. So there we were on that fine November morning, myself holding Fred's halter, Jeannie holding Penny's, camera slung over my back, when we were joined by Lama just as we had started to set off.

Monty in his time used to enjoy long walks, and he often came with us to Carn Barges. Lama never has done. Jeannie explains this by saying that Monty being born a suburban cat was innocent of country life dangers, while Lama born a wild cat was only too well aware of them. Anyhow I have never known her go beyond Minack boundaries; and that is part of the magic of her. Minack is her kingdom, and that is all she desires.

'I feel a bit guilty about her,' I said. Her presence produced a sense of competition . . . the donkeys were to be

115

the Christmas card, not Lama. And in any case she always looked vulnerable when she tried to join the donkeys on a walk, like a child trying to be grown up.

'She won't come far,' said Jeannie, 'she won't come any further than the top of the field.'

I led the way, Fred snorting and prancing in excitement, Jeannie a yard or two behind me with Penny, a gay matron of a Penny; and then a few yards behind them the cautious, determined Lama. We reached the field, and I had started to lead Fred down the slope when he suddenly stopped, pricked his ears in the direction of a jungle of grass, then lunged towards it while I tried to hold him back by his halter. And at that moment the grey cat darted out of the undergrowth. It dashed up the path we were coming down, past Jeannie and Penny, past Lama, then leapt to the left and raced down the other path towards the gate which stood at the top of our cliff meadows. Then disappeared underneath it.

'I haven't seen her for months and months,' said Jeannie.

'Why a "her"?'

'She's so small. She looks feminine.'

'Did you notice Lama?' I said, 'she behaved just like that other time a few weeks ago. Took no notice at all.'

I looked back again up the path, only for an instant, because Fred was pawing at the ground and jostling me and saying quite plainly that he wanted to move on. Lama had stopped, just as Jeannie said she would stop. She was sitting, watching us in detachment. She was certainly quite unperturbed by the commotion created by the presence of the little grey cat on her land.

The donkeys by the time they reached Carn Barges were in an amiable mood. We had not hurried. It was one of those unexpected mornings when, had I shut my eyes and possessed no sense of time, I would have believed it was a summer morning. The sun warmed my face and there was no breeze to cool it with a winter nip. Gulls flecked the grey rocks below us, and on the point that jutted out from our bay, quite still, a cormorant contemplated. On the other side of the little bay our meadows began to climb the cliff, and in a lower one, upright like a flagstaff, was the palm tree I planted when my mother died. Small meadows and strange shapes, high hedges sheltering them from the salt and the gales, they looked best in the winter. In the summer the undergrowth grew rampant, smothering the meadows with waist high green, making it difficult for strangers to believe that in early spring they were ablaze with daffodils. Now as we gazed at them they were neat. Geoffrey, Geoffrey who was with us years ago when we believed that new potatoes would prove our El Dorado and now was back with us, had scythed the meadows and trimmed the hedges; and now they were ready, bulbs beginning to stir, a climbing patchwork of hopeful expectation.

And up from the cliff, up the clear outline of the path which traced the big field, I could see Lama still where we left her. A black spot of a cat which for some reason, affection, curiosity, mild jealousy of the donkeys, wanted to wait for our return; as she had done so many times before. And when we had reached her again she would give us no fulsome greeting as a dog would have done; but instead would lazily stretch herself, begin to stroll slowly ahead of us and then, as if a joy suddenly swept through her, she would race away towards the cottage.

On the roof of the cottage, along its apex, I could see the pinpoints of the two gulls, Knocker and Squeaker. Their morning visit. It had become a habit of theirs to arrive about half past seven in the morning, force us to get up with their cries if we were not up already, stay until ten, disappear back to the rocks and the sea, and then return to the roof again an hour before dusk. But when the gales blew we never saw them until the storm had abated. Then they would appear again and we would be thankful it was over, one of us calling to the other: 'The gulls are back. The weather is on the mend!' and we would reward the gulls with home made bread.

Fred pushed his nose into my hand. He often did this when we were together, five minutes or so of munching grass and then a gesture of affection; and it was the same with Penny. Penny would watch Jeannie. If Jeannie started to move off the usual path, Penny would notice this and follow her. Both seemed to feel they were part of us. Something peaceful about it. Something secure. A subtlety. Not to be defined.

'Time to go back,' I said. I had tried to photograph them with ears pricked, biblical creatures with the rocks beside them in the foreground, and the sea far away below. But they had no interest in posing. Jeannie heaved them this way and that, trying to bring them together for the camera yet keeping them individually apart; and I had no idea whether I had pressed the button at the precise Christmas card moment.

'I'm ready to go,' said Jeannie. She said it in a tone of voice which set me wondering. As if she were impatient to return. Jeannie is the sort of person who will go silent when she is hiding her feelings; and although, in the process, she is apparently supporting me in whatever task I am pursuing, I am conscious of this silence. She is biding her time. She is reasoning that in due course, without causing any offence to me and without disclosing what is in her mind, she will gain her objective.

On this occasion, as we stood on Carn Barges and her eyes scanned our cliff meadows, she had an idea which she considered too fanciful to disclose to me.

It was an idea which resulted in the most tantalising story.

4

WE LEFT the donkeys in the stable meadow when we returned to Minack. Lama had waited for us as expected, raced
ahead to the cottage as was her custom, and had been rewarded for her patience by Jeannie with a saucer of fish.
Then, without saying anything to me, Jeannie disappeared.

I had some letters to write and as usual, being a slow
writer, they took much longer than I had hoped. Thus when
I looked at the clock, I realised suddenly that nearly an hour
had gone by and there was still no sign of her. It was unlike
her not to say what she was up to. We were close knit. If
there was a task to perform, an adventure to enjoy, we would
tell each other what it was we had in mind. Not in the
sense it was a duty to do so; for this breeds boredom. Just
for the fun of it. Why then had Jeannie not told me where
she had gone?

I finished my letters and walked out to a spot we called
the bridge, a bridge, that is of a ship. There was, however, no
possible similarity to such a bridge, except that we could
stand there, a few yards away up the slope from the cottage,
and view a vast expanse of moorland, sea and sky. We
seemed, metaphorically speaking, in command.

I was standing there when I heard Jeannie calling me,
then saw her running past the old stables, dark hair to her
shoulders, slim grey pants and dark blue polo neck jersey,
and shouting: 'Derek! Derek!' She was clearly highly
excited.

'Up here,' I said calmly, 'on the bridge.'

'You won't believe it,' she rushed out, 'it's the most extraordinary thing I've ever known!'

'What is?' I said in a matter of fact voice. I was a little irritated that she had disappeared for so long, and I did not feel in the mood to respond forthwith to her excitement.

'The grey cat is Lama's mother!'

It was a declaration. It was as if she were announcing that a visitor had arrived. I looked at her soothingly.

'You've been talking with the grey cat, I suppose, and she's told you this.'

'You're laughing at me!'

'I can hardly take you seriously.'

'You can give me a chance. You can listen to me.'

My teasing had reached stretching point.

'All right,' I said, 'go ahead. I'll listen.'

She had made a mental note, when Fred disturbed the grey cat and the latter ran away, that she disappeared under the small gate which topped our cliff; and that she ran in that direction with considerable purpose, as if she were going home. I too, of course, had seen her run that way but, as far as I was concerned, she was only escaping as quickly as she could from us. Jeannie, however, with her all embracing cat loving instincts, was curious. She was also, no doubt, wishing to indulge in the customary cat lover's pastime of trying to make friends with a stray.

And so after we had returned with the donkeys she had gone off to the cliff, through the gate and quietly down the steps, looking in one meadow and then into another. She then went down some further steps which brought her half way among the cliff meadows; one half climbing upwards to the big field, the other half falling to the rocks and the sea. At this point, a few yards off the path, there was a small cave. It was such a small cave that a human being could scarcely wriggle his way into it. It was more a crevice guarded by grey granite with a main entrance nearest the

120

path, and a slip of an exit, an escape route, at its far end. We had always been attracted by it. The interior was cosy, dry debris and rotted bracken like peat; and many times Jeannie and I had thought what a comfortable hideout it would have been for fox cubs; a much more suitable place than the bank not far away where cubs were reared year after year, always to be threatened by man when they were old enough to play.

Jeannie came to this cave and peered into it. She did so without thinking, a reflex action from our past talk about it. She had certainly not looked into it expecting to see the grey cat. She had to stoop, her knees touching the soil, in order to get a clear view; and as she did so she saw that the cave had an occupant. The occupant was neither the grey cat nor a fox cub.

It was a kitten. A black kitten.

'Good heavens,' I said.

'You see? Don't you see we've discovered where Lama came from? She was brought up in the cave by the grey cat.'

'Well,' I said cautiously, 'let's leave that fantasy for a moment. What did the kitten do when it saw you?'

'It ran away . . . up through the gap at the back.'

'Didn't you look for it?'

Jeannie being such a cat expert, so priding herself on understanding their ways and winning their confidence, must surely have caught the kitten.

'Of course I looked for it,' Jeannie exclaimed, though I observed a doubtful note in her voice, 'but it wouldn't have anything to do with me. In fact, I didn't see it again.'

I was, of course, sure that Jeannie was not fabricating the story. It was not her nature to do so, even as a joke. Hence I was bound to take her discovery seriously.

'How big was it?' I asked.

'Tiny . . . the size of your foot.'

'Only a few weeks old then?'

121

'Yes . . . perhaps a month or six weeks.'

'And no sign of any others?'

'Not a sign.'

Of course this *could* be the explanation as to where Lama came from. The grey cat was certainly known to us before Lama appeared; and for all we knew she may have been rearing kittens every year in the self-same cave without us being aware of it.

'Why on earth should there be only one kitten?' I asked, half to myself.

Jeannie was sitting beside me on a wood table we have on the bridge; and as we were talking we watched the Queen of the Isles, the new sister ship to the Scillonian, passing by on her way to the Scillies.

'There must be a sensible explanation,' I murmured again.

'Do we have to have one?'

'Well didn't you announce that the grey cat was Lama's mother?'

'Yes.'

'I'm only trying to think of evidence to prove it.'

'I wish,' said Jeannie, and at that moment I saw Lama strolling languidly towards us, 'I wish you wouldn't be so logical.'

'I'm not being logical. I'm only being sensible.'

'The same thing.'

'After all . . .'

'Of course we can't prove it,' Jeannie interrupted, 'I am only telling you what I *feel* is true.'

Lama had now come up to my gently swinging foot. She pushed her head softly against it, then looked up at me, trustingly, benignly, as if she were saying that she felt in a particularly loving mood and that she hoped I would respond. I did. I bent down and delicately touched her forehead to and fro.

'I tell you what we'll do,' I said, still stroking, 'we'll go down the cliff together, and I can see the kitten for myself.'

Lama, however, had no wish to see us leave. She was now purring, rubbing herself against my leg. A happy, peaceful Lama. No awareness that we were about to court a rival. No knowledge of the thoughts that were going through our minds, that we might at last have discovered her secret. Purr, purr, purr. She was the epitome of a contented cat. A houseful of comforts, endlessly admired, limitless hunting grounds, no enemies, so happy in her life that even the birds were safe. Purr, purr, purr.

'Wait a second,' said Jeannie, 'I'll put some bread and milk in a saucer. Better still, I'll put it in a jug and pour it out when we get down there.'

'And in the circumstances,' I said, 'Lama also deserves a special helping of something.' Then I added, feeling disloyal, 'It'll stop her from coming with us.'

There was a meadow with a hedge of elders, now bare of leaves, which lay above and to one side of the cave. It was a perfect place for us to hide; and so we went through the gate, down the steps, and stood there watching. We had only been there for a few minutes when I grew impatient, and I whispered to Jeannie that we should go straight down and look inside the cave. We had gone a few yards, moving very quietly, when suddenly the grey cat darted out of some undergrowth, raced towards the cave, and disappeared into the entrance.

'That's that,' I said, 'no use having a look now.'

'It would scare them still further if we did.'

Having been denied a sight of the kitten, I found my imagination awakened. Jeannie's excitement, I realised, was completely justified. And if when she first told me I reacted in a matter of fact fashion, I was now as keen as she was. I felt that here was an incident, an elusive fairy story which would have no end; and I was intrigued.

'If you wait here,' said Jeannie, 'I'll tip toe down to that trodden patch of earth near the entrance, and fill the saucer with bread and milk.'

I watched her do so, then when she returned, we went back to the hedge of elders, and waited. But there was no sign of grey cat or kitten. Only a robin flew down from a bush, had a look at the saucer, and flew back again.

'She knows we're here,' said Jeannie, 'she won't appear again until we've gone.'

We were never to see her or the kitten beside the saucer, but we soon realised it was going to help in another way. It acted as a marker, and while its contents were consumed we knew that they were still around. That first evening, when we went back, the saucer was empty, and Jeannie filled it up again. The same happened the following day, and the next. We would steal stealthily down the steps, hoping to catch them unawares but, although the bread and milk disappeared, our visits had obviously disturbed them. The kitten was no longer in the cave; or at any rate whenever we looked, it was empty.

On the fourth day the bread and milk was left untouched. So also on the fifth. We searched the two meadows closest to the cave but found no clue as to what might have happened; and the only sign of the kitten was a neat, round indentation in the dry debris and peat of the cave where she had lain curled asleep.

Thereupon we began blaming ourselves for having left food so close to their hiding place. We found the day dominated by our questions as to what might have happened; and the concern was for a kitten I had not yet even seen. I would find myself creeping through the gate and down the steps at various times of the day, to stare through the hedge, just to have a look at a saucer on the ground. Had they come back after all? Had the bread and milk been eaten?

On the Thursday, the third successive day that the saucer

had remained untouched, we regretfully decided the adventure was over. I would have to leave Jeannie alone with her satisfaction that she had seen the black kitten. A mystery that had momentarily titillated us, but would never be solved. A wild cat, and one small black kitten. There on the cliff amidst badgers roaming round them, gulls at night gathered on the rocks below, close together like still confetti, waves edging white round the darkness ceaselessly murmuring. We would leave them to this freedom.

That is what we thought. But on the Friday we were to realise that the grey cat had been watching *us*.

Plans had been made; and Lama was to be an ally in carrying them out.

5

AT FOUR o'clock on Friday afternoon we decided to take
the donkeys for a short walk. They had, in fact, hypnotised
us into doing so. They had been standing side by side at their
favourite spot in the field overlooking the cottage garden.
They were bored, and they communicated their boredom by
staring lugubriously at us when we went in and out of the
cottage; and, more effectively still, by impelling Jeannie to
watch them through the window as she sat in her armchair
enjoying a cup of tea.

'Let's take them to the onion meadow,' she said at last,
yielding as they had expected, to the stare. A lugubrious
stare never failed them. Sooner or later we were certain to
pay them attention.

We put on their halters and led them down the steep path
past the cottage, a hazardous few yards, for there within
reach was delectable escallonia, early flowering wallflower
plants, sweet williams, and various other delights which
favoured their fancy. We went on our way amid snorts and
other manifestations of donkey excitement; heads down to
the ground, for instance, with ears back, and frolicking,
harmless kicks. An adventurous time, as always at the beginning; a display of great pleasure, putting us both a little on
guard.

We turned right to the onion meadow, and instantly, I
who was leading Fred ahead of Jeannie and Penny, jabbed
at his halter; like jamming my foot on a brake. For there, a
few yards away along the path, her back to me, every line

126

of her eloquently describing her actions, was the grey cat. She was crouched. Her eyes were intent on couch grass ten feet from her. She was so certain of an impending capture that she was completely oblivious of our boisterous arrival.

'Hold it, Fred,' I said quietly. And then turning round towards Jeannie, I vigorously waved my hand telling her to stop. She had no need for such instructions. She too had seen the grey cat.

The donkeys did not approve of our sudden excitement. At one moment they were gaily setting off on a walk, the next they were returning whence they came. Why? This irrational behaviour on our part naturally vexed them, and when they again reached the gravel path by the cottage they anchored their hooves to the ground. A common gesture, of course, when a donkey is not doing what it wants. And it was only when Lama appeared, then collapsed upside down and coquettishly curled her paws to the sky a few yards away from them, that they were spurred once again to advance. The sight of her always entranced them.

'All right, donkeys,' said Jeannie soothingly when they were once more back in their field, 'we'll take you a long walk first thing tomorrow.' The promise did not impress them. They felt cheated.

But Jeannie and I were imbued with the enthusiasm of amateur detectives. We had been offered a clue and we were intent on following it up. If the grey cat was still roaming our land the chances were that the kitten could not be far away; and so if we could watch the grey cat, if we could shadow her movements, she might lead us to the new hide-out. So we now quickly returned to the spot where we had left her; and found her gone.

The light was now beginning to fail, and a wind from the south was rising. The sea was noisy, ominous, and fishing boats were hurrying across the bay towards Newlyn as if they were frightened of what was behind them. Blackbirds hoarsely chattered while they searched for roosting places, and gulls soared in the sky uttering human cries of warning. The magpies, over in the brush of the shadow valley, clattered their harsh sounds together like castanets; and looming above us, sweeping in from the sea, were the billowy dark clouds impatiently waiting to let loose their contents. A dirty night ahead. That was certain.

It was my idea that we should go down the cliff and have another look at the cave. I did not really expect to see anything, but the prospect of looking seemed to give us a purpose now that the grey cat had disappeared again. We went down the steps, glanced out of habit through the bare branches of the elder; and saw the grey cat, a few yards from the cave, sitting alertly with her back to us.

We were, of course, very surprised. Almost a week had gone by without a sign of her, and now within ten minutes we had seen her twice in widely separate places.

'She must have raced down from the path,' I said.

'She was probably in a hurry to take the mouse to the kitten.'

'She certainly went fast.'

'I'm *so* relieved,' said Jeannie, 'the kitten can't be far away.'

We were content, as it was getting dark, to leave it at that. If we decided to search for the new hideout, we would do so tomorrow; and so we went back up the steps to the field. At the top of the steps to the left, there is what is called the skol meadow, and beyond it there is another meadow where grew a patch of soleil d'or. Only a few of them and not enough to send away commercially, but as they were the earliest bulb flowers of all they gave us much pleasure. Here was spring before even winter had begun, and from time to time we would stroll to the meadow and see how the green spikes were progressing. We did so on this occasion. A whim on Jeannie's part took us there despite the growing darkness; and it was five to six minutes before we got back to the big field and had reached the path which led us fifty yards to the cottage.

Two or three yards up the path, close to the left hand bank, we saw Lama. It was not unusual for her to be there. It was her sentry box. She would post herself at this spot, awaiting our return, whenever she had spied us going off for a walk and had been too late to catch up with us. There she was, a black shadow in the gloom, about to receive a loving, rapturous greeting from Jeannie and me, when suddenly I saw her leap a couple of feet in the air, heard her utter a jungle battle cry, then watched her disappear at speed up the path towards the cottage. The sound of battle cries faded; and all was silent again, except for the rising wind.

'I don't think,' said Jeannie, 'that all that noise and fuss seemed very genuine.' A cat connoisseur's remark. An experienced observer's assessment of a situation which was suspect. Lama had put on a show. A flamboyant temper had been meant to impress us. A cacophony of empty meaning noise, a sawdust gesture of bravery, a display of feline exhibitionism aimed at pulling the wool over our eyes. The *other* cat, so the elaborate pretence went, was *not* a friend. *That* is why I am chasing it.

But while Jeannie sensed what had happened, I had seen. I had been a little ahead of her, caught sight of Lama, and simultaneously had observed her companion, and they were side by side, a black shadow and a grey one. It was bewildering.

'Unless I'm dotty,' I said, 'it's the grey cat again.'

'It can't be.'

'What she's been doing racing up and down from the cliff like this is beyond my comprehension.'

'And Lama behaving like that!'

'We'll see if we can find them.'

We hurried up the path, and first went to look in the old

stables, which we often referred to as the Lama House. It was Jane and Shelagh who invented the name, because they believed that Lama sometimes used to shelter there when she was wild. It was an ancient building with a battered stable door, and there was a gap at the base through which she could have entered, even when the door was shut. Opposite the door, facing the lane, were two small windows but even with the light from these, and the door open, it was still dark inside. For most of the year we used it as a store place, a dumping spot for unneeded machines, bags of fertilisers, and anything else we wanted to lose sight of. But when the hard weather came, the donkeys sheltered there, and hay covered the cobbled stones of the floor, and the feet thick walls were ramparts against the bitter wind.

There was no trace of Lama, and we went outside again, and across to the trees on the other side of the lane beside the greenhouse. The donkeys caught sight of us in the dark and Fred began to trumpet a song, then Penny joined in with her terrible groaning contralto. No duet could be less musical yet more romantic. Through time the world has heard the sad calls of the donkeys. A bewailing sound, a miserable sound; but, for those who wish to hear it, it is also the sound of defiance and of the triumph of long suffering.

'She's here!' I heard Jeannie suddenly shout, 'and what's more the grey cat is on a branch just above her!'

It was an old elm, spreading its branches behind the packing shed, a fat trunk in which green woodpeckers had chiselled nestholes over the years.

'But they look friendly!' I said in surprise when I saw them.

They were within paw striking distance of each other, ten feet from the ground, Lama balancing on one branch while the grey cat was just above her, her tail encircling the branch she was sitting on like a monkey. They were watching each other, dozily, no sign of animosity. They were not even stirred into action by our upturned faces. No imaginary temper this time. They were clearly content in each other's company. Indeed Lama was rubbing her head against the branch in such a way that she appeared to be purring; but this we could not hear because of the wind rushing through the trees.

We put Boris to bed, shutting the door of his house in the wood and bidding him good night as he sat on his perch, then we went indoors. We had not been there long before Jeannie's curiosity got the better of her, and she picked up the torch, and went back again to look up at the tree. They were there still, communing with each other, a few feet apart; and when Jeannie shone the torch directly on the grey cat, she showed no fear. She was a little cat; a neat, small head, a short body, and the plush fur of the semi-Persian. There was no doubt in Jeannie's mind of the similarity. It had started to spatter with rain, and the wind was growing angry, and the sea was beginning to roar. But up there in the tree Lama and the grey cat continued their silent, feline conversation.

'Have we solved your secret at last?' said Jeannie by herself to Lama in the darkness. 'Have we?'

It is easy to smile at those who gain stability from the love of an animal; but they are only being sincere. Trust is being given to trust, an antidote to the pace of life. They are rebelling against the standards of the herd, the superficial fashions currently in vogue. Instead of being greedy, deceptive, envious and slick, they are simply responding to affection. The secret heart receives its yearning.

Lama returned to the cottage in due course, and she spent the night curled at the bottom of the bed. In the morning the wind and the rain were still lashing the windows, making a noise like the rattle of drums; and I was good-naturedly annoyed when Jeannie said to me after breakfast that she was making a stew . . . and would I fetch an onion from the string in the stables?

I put a raincoat over my shoulders and ran down the path; and my hand was on the bottom part of the stable door to open it, when I saw something inside on an old sack in the middle of the cobblestone floor.

Asleep on the sack was the black kitten.

6

WE WERE living again the time when Lama first came to Minack. A black cat in the offing, uninvited, imposing its personality upon us from a distance. No Jane and Shelagh this time to help Jeannie in her manoeuvres. No vacancy for a cat to fill.

Hence, although my first reaction was to hasten to tell Jeannie, my second was one of vague concern. A kitten which had arrived in such a magical fashion could not be denied a home; and what would Lama say to that? I doubted, too, my own behaviour. Lama had taken the place of Monty in my life, and I viewed with apprehension the prospect of having to divide my loyalties. I was still a one cat man.

I was, however, anticipating a situation which had not yet matured. I was so enchanted by the thought of the kitten clambering up the steps of the cliff and on up the steep field towards the stables that I was taking it for granted that the journey had been made with a purpose; and the purpose was to win our approval. So also thought Jeannie.

'Easy now to understand why the grey cat came to see Lama,' she said. I guessed what she was thinking. The situation provided excellent material for her fantasy weaving. 'She asked permission,' Jeannie went on, 'for the kitten to stay at Minack.'

'Booking accommodation from the landlady?' I joked.

'Very funny.'

'So you think Lama has agreed to share her home?'

'Some understanding took place.'

'Rubbish,' I said, 'anyhow, come and see it.'

We went down to the stables and Jeannie once again hopefully carried a saucer of bread and milk; but when we reached the stable door I foolishly coughed, and the kitten woke up and, with the instant reaction of an animal caught off guard, dashed into a corner under a fat bale of peat. We made no attempt to lure it out, for not even Jeannie expected to be friends straight away. Its confidence had to be slowly won. It would have to be the same story as that of Lama; the growing trust, won not by a gimmick but by time.

'Put the saucer down just here,' I said, 'and we'll go round to the lane and watch through the window. The kitten will be in our sight.'

I had never before watched a hungry, wild black kitten, the size of my foot, ecstatically devour a saucer of bread and milk. There had been no pause, no frightened wait for us to disappear. We walked round the building and looked through the window, and in those few seconds the kitten had made up its mind. Fear was not going to interfere with hunger. And so when we put our faces to the glass there was this tiny black daisy of a face hugging the saucer, tiny pink tongue shooting at its contents.

'It's so small,' I said, 'do you think it could have walked here on its own? I wonder if the mother carried it?'

'We will never know,' said Jeannie.

Small as it was we could see the resemblance to Lama. The neat little head, the short body, the firm cup handle of a tail, and the black velvet of its fur.

'When it grows up,' I said doubtfully, 'we won't be able to tell the difference between the two of them.'

'Your tone suggests you're regretting it.'

'I'm only thinking . . . '

'I know what you're thinking,' said Jeannie, laughing,

'it's always the same with you . . . shying away from a new arrival. Just as you did with Monty and the donkeys, and Lama for that matter. It's your nature to be like this in the beginning.'

'Oh, well,' I said, 'it's only that I can't help wondering how Lama is going to like sharing her kingdom.'

But Lama's mood during the coming days could not be faulted. I had foreseen the possibility that she might storm the stables and put the kitten to flight. There was nothing to stop her doing so except her good nature, the gap in the door was still open as we had no wish to cage the kitten inside; and so the kitten, so to speak, was at her mercy. Lama, however, seemed not to be aware of it. She pursued her customary peregrinations. She fenced with Boris. She dozed in the packing shed. She helped Jeannie to bunch freesias by pushing her head in the blooms as they lay on the bench. She displayed no sign of knowing that there was a possible heir apparent within miaowing distance. There was, in fact, an air about her which suggested she was a lady sure of her position. No threats from anywhere, let alone from a kitten.

Nor did the kitten behave in the way we expected. Instead of responding to our attention, it hid from us. We would arrive at the stable door, look inside, and be just in time to see the tiny figure dash to its fortress; a fortress built from the bale of peat, sacks of fertilisers, an old table, a disused motor hoe, and a bundle of wooden stakes. Out of sight and out of reach, it was as safe as a rabbit in its warren, and it would only emerge to eat the food we had left for it, long after we had gone. We would watch through the window, half an hour or more, before we saw it creep from its hiding place to the saucer.

After ten days of such behaviour I began to feel thwarted. Moreover the kitten was forcing us to lead a double life; and so when Lama came purring round us we both had a guilty conscience. What right had we to flirt with a wild kitten

135

when Lama was so trusting? We had done our best to win its affection but it had spurned us. It clearly did not want our company. And if that were the case, so we argued, we could justifiably attempt to satisfy our curiosity. We would open up the fortress and see the kitten at close quarters.

On the December morning that we decided to reach the kitten's hiding place, Lama's attitude suddenly became frivolous. We walked out of the cottage and found her skittishly playing with a pebble from the gravel; and before we could stop her, she dashed gaily down the path to the stable door.

'Now there's going to be trouble,' I said.

'You stop here,' said Jeannie, 'I'll catch her.'

Lama, however, had no intention of being caught; and as soon as Jeannie approached her, she jumped on the wall out of reach.

'Let her be,' I said, feeling guilty again that we were deceiving her, 'I'll block up the gap in the door . . . and so the kitten won't get out and Lama won't get in.'

We quietly began dismantling the fortress. The motor hoe was lifted out first, then the old table, and after that the bundle of wooden stakes.

'I should say it is behind the gap between the peat and the fertiliser bags,' I said, realising I had now to be on guard. The heavy part of the moving was about to begin.

'Be careful.'

'I will.'

I shifted the bale of peat about eighteen inches; and I pushed aside first one, then a second bag. I had moved enough to see the corner which we believed was the fortress. It was empty.

'It hasn't dashed away while I was moving this?'

'I can't see it.'

Only the previous evening Jeannie had taken it some chopped liver and, as she was about to go through the door-

136

way, it had brushed her leg in the dark.

'It's not here,' I said, 'there's not a sign of it here.'

At this moment there was a rattle behind me. Lama was poised like an acrobat on the edge of the stable door. A black cat edged against the daylight. A cat, which a second later, was on the cobblestones on the floor beside us; an upturned tummy of a black cat, white whisker distinct among the luxuriant others, a happy black cat.

'Why so coquettish, Lama?' I said, bending down and stroking her. Then I paused, and turned to Jeannie, laughing. 'Do you know,' I said, 'I believe you were right, Jeannie.'

'How?'

'Lama has been making fools of us.'

'I never said that.'

'You said that the grey cat was Lama's mother, and that she asked Lama a favour concerning the kitten.'

'I said that more or less.'

'That's what *did* happen, I reckon. Lama agreed to let the kitten stay in the stables until it grew strong enough to go away and find a home of its own.'

'You ridiculed me when I suggested it.'

'I take it all back. But there's one thing I want to know ... what has happened to the grey cat?'

We had not seen her since that night when she was in the tree. It was indeed many weeks before we saw her again.

'She felt her kitten was safe. She could do no more for it, so she went off. After all Lama was safe after she came here ...'

Lama had had enough attention, and had got up, and was sauntering away.

'Dear Jeannie,' I said, as we also moved off from the stables, 'I'm glad you've got a fey mind.'

'Are you laughing again?'

'Certainly not. A fey mind makes unreasonable facts convincing.'

'Well,' said Jeannie, unsure whether I was paying a compliment, 'whatever my mind may be, there is a job of work to be done. We must send out the Christmas cards today. Will you help?'

'Certainly.'

'Let's go.'

As we went up the path, we passed Lama. She was sitting on a rock, a huge rock embedded in the ground, a rock which had been anchored there through the ages. She sat with tip of tail flicking, her oriental eyes blinking serenely; and, had it not been for the breeze, I would have heard her purrs.

A cat with a mission achieved.

WE WERE alone at Christmas. Jeannie's mother had died three years ago; and Angus three months before her. We were alone except for Boris and the gulls, the donkeys and Lama; and the kitten we never saw.

It was still in the neighbourhood, no doubt about that. Every evening after Lama had come indoors, Jeannie would go out into the darkness and leave a saucer in the stables. It didn't matter how stormy the night, she still kept her appointment. Her task was performed, she said, because of Lama. A question of two cats from the cliff.

And now on this Christmas morning, Lama herself was about to perform an important duty. I was lying comfortably in bed when I heard Jeannie call from the sitting room: 'Lama is coming to you with a present!' Then I heard her add urgently in a whisper: 'Go on Lama! No, not that way . . . through the door!'

Then Lama appeared, almost at eye level, and I observed that around her silky black neck was a red ribbon; and attached to the ribbon, dangling against her chest was a decorated narrow box which suggested the container of a fountain pen. It was indeed.

'Lama . . . thank you!' I said, grabbing her, and lifting her on to the bed and holding her, firm hand on soft fur, 'just what I want.'

This was the game of Christmas. The relish of absurdities which enrich momentarily the act of giving; and within a few minutes of Lama's presentation I was up. I pulled a thick jersey over my dressing gown. I did not bother about socks as I pulled on my Wellington boots. Then I was off into the chill morning to fetch the donkeys, collecting on my way the two placards I had already prepared. The placards were the lids of old cardboard flower boxes; and on one I had scrawled MERRY CHRISTMAS! and on the other WITH LOVE FROM US BOTH. I hung the first around Fred's neck, the second around Penny's; and on each was attached a large envelope.

'Come and see the donkeys!' I shouted when I had led them back to the cottage.

'Hurry Jeannie!'

I had pushed them ahead of me, and I feared they might become restless as they stood on their own by the porch, two shaggy heads side by side waiting to deliver their presents. Nothing very important. A silk scarf from each.

'Donkeys!' cried Jeannie, 'whatever have you been up to?'

At this moment Knocker and Squeaker the gulls on the roof began crying, pointing their beaks to the heavens, screeching a demand for attention.

'Here . . . give them these cheese rinds,' said Jeannie handing me a plate over Fred's head. And as she did so he tried to push his big nose into it.

'Not for *you* Fred,' I said, and threw the pieces on to the roof.

They both had their reward soon after, and when I took them back to the field they were still munching the carrots Jeannie had given them. I shut the gate, watched them amble away, then hurried down to the wood to let Boris out of his house.

I was late, and he was cross that I had kept him waiting; and I heard him hissing before I had even turned the key in the lock. 'Sorry Boris,' I said, as I opened the door, 'it's Christmas. Merry Christmas old Boris!' He came out of the house flapping his wings and followed me back, waddling from side to side until he reached his pond in front of the packing shed. He always had his breakfast there, nowhere else would do; and I gave him a handful of corn. He pushed his beak into it, and waggled his tail feathers in delight.

On the way back to the cottage I had a look in the stables, and saw that the saucer of bread and milk had been left untouched. Usually it was clean by the morning.

'No kitten last night,' I said when I returned.

'That's the second night running,' said Jeannie, 'it'll be back tonight.' It was true that we had noticed that the food could go untouched for two nights but was always eaten on the third.

'It's still looking for a vacancy,' went on Jeannie, 'and until it finds one it will always come back.'

'Well,' I said smiling, thinking of the old lady in Penzance who, when Monty died, assured me the vacancy would soon be filled, 'let's have breakfast and then go a wandering walk around Minack with the cat which *did* find a vacancy.'

Lama, fortunately, was in the mood for a walk, and as we moved off towards the cliff she kept only a yard or so behind us. There were to be no delays on her part on this occasion. She wanted to remain close to us, jauntily enjoying herself, finding a feline delight in sharing the pleasure of the day with us. And when we reached the cliff gate she dashed ahead underneath it, like the grey cat had done that day when Fred had disturbed her.

'Back where she came from,' I said to Jeannie, watching Lama scamper down the steps. Then I added: 'You remember how Monty never liked coming down here.'

'But Monty,' replied Jeannie, 'was not born within sound of the sea.'

The only entrance to our cliff was through this gate at the top. It was no place for strangers. There was a deep cleft biting into the land, a sheer fall to the sea below, guarding one boundary of the meadows; and the other boundary disappeared into boulders, brambles, gorse and, in summer, a forest of bracken. Below were the rocks, granite and blue elvin pitted with fissures, huge ungainly shapes each part of the whole which sloped without plan inevitably to the sea. Here the seaweed, draped like an apron, thickened the water at low tide; and gulls, oyster catchers, and turnstones poked among it, uttering wild cries. There was the sense of loneliness, and yet of greatness. This was unmanageable nature, the freedom man chases.

And to us the cliff reflected our endeavour since we came to Minack. It was a part of ourselves. We had seen it those years ago when it was untamed, and visioned the meadows we would carve from the undergrowth, the rich crops we would grow, the sure future we would build. Here we had been a part of some victories and many defeats. We had seen harvests of early potatoes lashed by a gale and destroyed in a night. We had laboured on hot summer days on this cliff shovelling with the long handled Cornish spade beneath the potato plants, Jeannie on hands and knees picking up the potatoes and filling the sacks, then the long steep climb to the top, a sack at a time, journey after journey.

We had rejoiced in the flower season at the sight of the daffodils, dazzling yellow against the blue sea, gulls high above, gannets plummeting offshore; then gladly endured the steady task of picking, gathering an armful and slowly filling a basket; and the climb again, heavy basket in either hand. Such as this was our victory. Here in remoteness, a sense of communion with the base of beauty. Not victory in a worldly sense. We produced. We were two of the losing originals. When our efforts left our environment, so did our control. Far away people, cool in their calculations, undisturbed by our hopes, beset with their own problems, decreed our reward.

We had our shield. Moments like the quiet of a Christmas morning when Jeannie and I were together, with a cat called Lama who was born within the sound of the sea.

NEL BESTSELLERS

NEL P.O. BOX 11, FALMOUTH TR10 9EN, CORNWALL:

For U.K.: Customers should include to cover postage, 19p for the first book plus 9p per copy for each additional book ordered up to a maximum charge of 73p.

For B.F.P.O. and Eire: Customers should include to cover postage, 19p for the first book plus 9p per copy for the next 6 and thereafter 3p per book.

For Overseas: Customers should include to cover postage 20p for the first book plus 10p per copy for each additional book.

Name ....

Address ....

....

Title ....
(NOVEMBER)